Karma

How to Improve the Quality of Your Life

(How Karma Can Be Burnt Up Through Proper Meditation)

Dakota Lowe

Published By **Elena Holly**

Dakota Lowe

All Rights Reserved

Karma: How to Improve the Quality of Your Life (How Karma Can Be Burnt Up Through Proper Meditation)

ISBN 978-1-77485-921-6

No part of this guidebook shall be reproduced in any form without permission in writing from the publisher except in the case of brief quotations embodied in critical articles or reviews.

Legal & Disclaimer

The information contained in this ebook is not designed to replace or take the place of any form of medicine or professional medical advice. The information in this ebook has been provided for educational & entertainment purposes only.

The information contained in this book has been compiled from sources deemed reliable, and it is accurate to the best of the Author's knowledge; however, the Author cannot guarantee its accuracy and validity and cannot be held liable for any errors or omissions. Changes are periodically made to this book. You must consult your doctor or get professional medical advice before using any of the suggested remedies, techniques, or information in this book.

Upon using the information contained in this book, you agree to hold harmless the

Author from and against any damages, costs, and expenses, including any legal fees potentially resulting from the application of any of the information provided by this guide. This disclaimer applies to any damages or injury caused by the use and application, whether directly or indirectly, of any advice or information presented, whether for breach of contract, tort, negligence, personal injury, criminal intent, or under any other cause of action.

You agree to accept all risks of using the information presented inside this book. You need to consult a professional medical practitioner in order to ensure you are both able and healthy enough to participate in this program.

TABLE OF CONTENTS

Introduction 1

Chapter 1: How Vibrations Function In The Both The Worlds Of The Unseen And The Seen. 4

Chapter 2: How The Law Vibration Can Change Your Life For The Better 9

Chapter 3: The Secret Of Intentionality.. 20

Chapter 4: Solo Versus Group Vibration. 32

Chapter 5: Create Your Own "Vibration Repeater Chamber" 45

Chapter 6: Basic Rules 51

Chapter 7: Different Types Of Theft 74

Chapter 8: Types Of Speech 113

Chapter 9: Karma Theory 135

Conclusion 183

Introduction

If you are worried about money, will you get money?

Most of the time, things get worse, aren't they?

If you thought of what you would like to buy Did you ultimately decide to purchase it?

When you consider the hurtful things people did to you, wouldn't you become more anxious? Don't your relationships get even more strained?

If you are focused on a specific issue, does it begin to look like a complete failure in the shortest time? Does it not seem like it is heavy?

Have you ever woken up thinking about someone and then had that person contact to you at the end of the night?

In case any one of these preceding resonates with you, be at ease knowing that your brain is not fooling you.

Welcom to the realm of VIBRATION.

Every thought you transmit to the world is a sound.

It's not just about transmitting vibrations to the universe - these can have an impact on your surroundings as well as the universe.

Does this sound like hippy? All boils down to the physics.

Physics researchers have long recognized that the things that appear real and solid are actually broken to smaller pieces which are then reduced more into wave.

Yes, the strongest piece of steel is composed of iron alloyed with other metals , and blended with carbon.

Break these molecules and you'll have Atoms.

Smash atoms into protons, neutrons and electrons

When you break them down, you'll have subatomic particles similar to quarks.

Each level in this structure, we observe increasing amounts of empty space

It turns out that the majority of those things we see as real, immovable, solid fixable... can be actually made out by empty space.

As sub-atomic particles get broken down, they're vibrating energy packets.

The thoughts you think of are creating into packets that appear empty or appear to be invisible...

However, just like subatomic vibrations, they're extremely real.

As waves in the surface of a pond, they radiate outwards, and then reflect in the opposite direction...

Your thoughts can have consequences that manifest in many ways.

Your thoughts are the vibrations you send to the universe. .... the existence you're living is the direct result of the way you transmit signals to the rest of the universe.

This book teaches you about how vibrations function and how you can utilize them to your advantage.

The answer isn't to ignore your personal vibration to the universe , but learn to be in SYMPHONY with the universe.

Chapter 1: How Vibrations Function In The Both The Worlds Of The Unseen And The Seen.

You might be thinking that the universe is composed of liquids, solids, gases and various other physical forms. They are physical forms that you are able to see using your sight as well as your sense of hearing as well as smell, taste and even touch. This is the way that most people view reality. If you had to dismantle the entirety of everything, you will find lots of empty space. Many of the things you believe to be solid and real that can help you, protect you or even do something for you, but this is a vast empty space. If you reduce things to the simplest level there is no distinction between energy and matter. The whole thing could be reduced to forms of waves. Waves break through and bounce.

When you speak in a space the only reason people hear your voice is due to the sound waves you have sent out, and the air is disturbed. The air's movement is reflected by the eardrums of those around and they interpret it as sound. Similar to that, if you're in a specific area of room and you talk your words, the sound waves you released bounced back at you. This is referred to as echo. A dynamic call and response takes place. You broadcast the waves, and it the waves bounce back at you. Does this sound familiar? It should. What do you receive? You will get a response. Did you consider the fundamental process? You've probably figured out the way in which the universe reacts.

It is a mystery to many and seems like the universe could be composed of very basic components and simple dynamic. One of them is the idea of action and response that could take the form of calls and responses, waves, etc. It's crucial to start by understanding this principle, and I'm hoping I don't disappoint you. It's extremely easy. As you are standing somewhere and you transmit an indication and the signal is returned. It may not be in the exact shape, but it does come back. Following is wave activity. The activity of waves is determined by the frequency and wavelength of waves. All colors you can see around you. They are just light waves.

It has different wavelengths from brown, which is distinct from red. These apparent distinctions boil down to one wavelength. Are you with me this far? That's most of what you see from outside. Similar to when you hear an ambulance approaching. The sound fades and then as it gets close to your home, it sounds it in a loud way, however as it gets away, it fades. This is known as"the Doppler effect. It's interestingly enough, it's tempting to believe that sound waves aren't as tangible than the seat sits on. In the end, they don't appear in a tangible form, right? However, concentrated or intense waves are able to break through even the most difficult materials.

The kidney stone sufferers are happy that this is the case. Why? When patients undergo Shockwave therapy there is no physical object placed in their kidneys to eliminate the stones. The surgeon does not cut open the kidneys to let the sludge out and then take out the stones. Instead, a device releases sound waves which crush the kidney stones. The kidneys then absorb the stones pushed through your urinary tract. This is how powerful, concentrated waves can be. The effectiveness of the wave is all down to focusing on the correct frequency range of the wave.

When the Shockwave device for therapy is tuned at the incorrect frequency, it's not doing its job. These are just a few examples of waves that exist in our natural environment. They aren't just floating around in the air. There is no neutrality in them. They may work for you or against you. They exist. We are now in the same boat, I would like you to look at your thoughts. Your thoughts are vibrations within the same frequency. Like radio waves, it is impossible to think about your thoughts.

You can't touch them you can't smell them, touch them, as well as taste them however they're there. When you read this book numerous thoughts come to your brain. While you're thinking and creating thoughts, you're creating waves. It's within a specific frequency range. You're not aware. Different people have differently and have different thoughts, which differ in the frequency they use. The most interesting part is all this. As I said earlier the vibrations, waves and in turn waves aren't neutral. They have an impact on.

Thoughts are not immune to this. Your thoughts generate vibrations with similar frequency. Also your life is the reflection of your thoughts. Before we move on into chapter two and get into the practical implications of this, I want to clarify the meaning of thoughts that are vibrations, waves, thoughts and all other things. You might be thinking this is a kind of metaphysical hocus-pocus. You may think that I've just carried this whole thing out.

Well, in physics , there is a theory that aims to explain all things in the universe. It's not completely developed yet, but there are many aspects to it that physicists are all on. It's known as string theory. String theory defines the universe as a whole made up of waves and vibrations. There is a science behind this. It's real. Whatever your beliefs are, whether in a god or a metaphysical Being, we can trust it is true that science claims that everything is traceable to waves or vibrations. Since we're at the same level, be seeing you in chapter 2.

Chapter 2: How The Law Vibration Can Change Your Life For The Better

After you have wrapped your mind around the idea that everything is a wave. How can this have a real-world impact on your daily life? How will this knowledge affect your life to your advantage? The failure of your goals guilt, regret, or uncertainty are a result of the lack of understanding about how the thoughts and vibrations you broadcast to the universe form your reality. As if you've got this power of which you are unaware of, and you're left to be afraid or feel guilty due to the consequences of this power. Through your life you're not aware that you've been positioned in accordance to the tune you are constantly playing within your mind. It is because of a basic concept, which is explained below.

The world is manifested around you, based on your frequency of vibration

Different people emit waves in various frequency ranges. You're a radio station. You're broadcasting an e-signal to the universe and everyone else within your vicinity does exactly the same. By using different frequencies. This is the reason for the different patterns between our daily lives. It also shows that you're not inactive. It is possible that you think you're not doing anything in your own life or maybe you're convinced that whatever you do, it doesn't do any change that can alter your life in a positive way. But, think twice.

By thinking that you can improve or preserve your universe. It is the truth that because of the energy of your vibrations you're not only a passive subject to what the world throws at you. What you get is directly the result of the vibrations that you transmit. Also, since you create, regardless of whether you're happy or not, and you're aware of it, and whether you're aware or not, you are a part of the world. Everything that occurs within your existence is the result of the energy you're emitting. Call and respond. Echoes are everywhere. Where does that the sound comes from? The signal is reflected back to you, based on the frequency you're listening to.

Thoughts can trigger other thoughts

When we broadcast loudly to the world through your thoughts, the world responds by a feedback, it may be an echo, or it could be something else and you continue by rethinking your thoughts. The thing that is odd about it all. Thoughts never remain completely neutral. They reflect your perspective or your station for transmission which has an agenda or a particular perspective on reality and organizing it. Even if you're unaware of it doesn't mean it's untrue. Even if you didn't acknowledge it does not mean that this won't impact your life. Do not think for a moment that if you ask you to broadcast messages and get them back from others, that you're not transformed. There is a lot happening in your head due to this process.

Thoughts are ingrained into your brain via the repetition of thoughts and their ubiquitousness

Ubiquity signifies that it's everywhere. Your thoughts you send out and get in return from your universe is exactly the identical. What's happening is that the inner reality, your beliefs are getting strengthened. In the end, you begin seeing everything in relation to or in relation to the beliefs you have already established. According to the old saying"When you're a Hammer, the world's problems begin becoming like nails. Don't be shocked that by repetitive use, everything in the world begins to appear as an expression of your values that makes sense to you as well as what your priorities are and what your ideals could be. All of this comes as a unexpected.

The most interesting aspect of all this. Your thoughts are reflected in the reactions of the universe. Thoughts are not completely neutral. They create something, and when the universe responds, the majority times, you do not be aware of the full spectrum of reactions or the full image. Why? It is because you can only discern these responses based on the environment you are in. Also you are able to only discern or comprehend the answers the world offers you based on the way you think. Do you think you are an individual who has won? Do you believe everything can be achieved, that every obstacle lies an opportunity and do you think that people are naturally good?

Are you convinced that people are inherently evil and always motivated by self-interest? Do you think you are as a victim? Each of these scenarios reveal different mental models. If you emit a vibration of the world and get the world responds you will be able to interpret and interpret the echo in accordance with your perspective. It is only possible to make sense of the world's response by analyzing the frequency you set. The more you experience this process and the more you confirm the things you believe you already have learned regarding the universe. It's a repeated pattern. If you've got an open mind, or you're aware of the situation it is possible to allow this procedure to reprogram the brain. It will require some time on your own. It is important to be aware of the procedure.

The way your subconscious alters your reality

The world is basically neutral. It's an awe-inspiring thought to lots of people, particularly those who believe that there is a war going on or has something to do with it. If you believe you're the victim each word you speak can be a bullet. Every glance is a type of weapon. It's easy to feel small and powerless, helpless placed on the margins of your eyes.

That's the reality you have. It's how you choose to view reality. However, if you consider it an impartial race I don't think you'd believe me.

Imagine a burning building with bright orange-yellow flames. smoke is escaping from the building, and people are in the top floors shouting their lungs out. Help! Help!. There are more in the basement of the building who are running. The sweat that is coming out from under the skin. The eyes go down, their mouths open and they scream in silence. When you look at that scene and your mind's "radio station" is tuned at the level of "worst-case scenario" where everything becomes an emergency, and everything will lead to the death of the world. What do you think you'll respond? You're likely to be terrified. It's possible that things hit you so intensely that you don't even take the time to think about it.

You can remove your phone and make a call to an emergency number to the department. However it is the case that your frequency settings "everything is possible to solve". How would you deal with that? You wouldn't allow the anxiety of others take over you. You shouldn't let your emotions be affected by the turmoil of everyone else's. Instead you'll decide that since your frequency setting states that everything is manageable with a simple solution you'll pull off your phone and make contact with the fire department. Then place yourself in the area to assist firefighters as they arrive with a firetruck. So, let me ask you this question: what frequency setting do you believe will benefit the people trapped or running from the building most? It's a simple choice. That's why choice of frequency settings is. In the end, your subconscious or radio station's frequency, it's your reality. I'll go over this in the discussion below.

Your subconscious is the one who edits your reality

It all starts in neutral conditions. As I've described in the context that follows, there are at a minimum two possible ways to interpret any given situation. In any set of external stimuli there are at minimum two possibilities. It begins with stimuli, that are then processed through your brain. This is the way you program your mind to perceive " the reality". What are the outcomes? Thoughts. These are your thoughts about the world. Then you give them to others to the world.

What happens? Then it comes back with the exact format that you sent them out.

That is you're assigned to a specific frequency range, and what you receive falls within that range. This shouldn't come as a surprise since you are able to only receive signals that fall within the range you set. The universe is can see, but you're only getting a tiny part of it. What does your mind think when you think it's a confirmation of what you believe you already are aware of. Your conscious brain believes that this is the truth. It's real because it's returning.

It is merely confirmation of the things we thought previously. The subconscious acts as reinforcement. If you encounter the same stimuli it does the exact process. This interprets real-world events in a particular way , and that creates an emotions. You tell yourself this is the reason I believe things to be , and it's not always neutral. It triggers an emotional reaction. If you are emotionally overwhelmed, you are more likely to perform certain actions.

What do you believe will occur if your actions coincide with your mental state? The same will happen as when you make a decision there are usually consequences , and this can trigger stimuli that then create thoughts, and it's repeated repeatedly. The whole process gets stronger with each repetition , unless you're vigilant and aware that this is the way you alter your perception of reality. All it takes is the radio receiver station. What frequency do you belong to? What do you think? It's selected.

The positive news

You're always in control and is a shock to many who believe that they are a hard worker and plan your work regardless of your efforts it's impossible to get everything written up. It's like getting into the same bad relationship every time. However, even if you're in a relationship in a relationship with a different partner. It appears that regardless of the effort you've put into something similar to your job, it hasn't felt as satisfying or soiled like you'd have imagined.

It's as if there's no way to be completely in control, and your life appears to be the film that's playing before you and all you're able to do is sit and look away from the screen. It's how it appears. This is the frequency range you've selected. In reality, it's totally different. You have chosen to be in that particular wavelength. You are able to easily change the dial to a different wavelength range. It's a way to the control. You are able to choose your attitude and in turn you can decide on your thoughts.

Once you change your attitude The chain reaction mentioned above won't need to be working against you. It is able to work for you. It is repeated several times and gets stronger and more powerful every time. In the end, it manifests itself in the action. It is possible that the action you choose to decide to take isn't that significant. If you begin doing activities that are different from what you do every day What do you believe will take place? You'll get different results. All the worry, complaining, bellyaching and worry won't alter the reality of your life in the event that your behavior doesn't change.

Let's make one thing crystal clear. The world does not care about the way you feel or motives, or motives. They're all good, but everyone has these. What is it that the world is paying an eye to and what the world cannot ignore, but needs to take a seat and pay attention? Actions. As powerful as your feelings may be, when you take action on them, they begin to change. This is when the world reacts. There are consequences, and these effects are caused by the stimuli I continue to talk about. If you've changed your radio frequency to match the one of your mentality Things begin to change for you. You start scaling up and alter the direction. Could that be simple? Absolutely it wouldn't be. Does it happen in one day? No. If you're looking to make positive changes it is important to realize how you're in charge. You control your mindset. You are able to change the channel to a different wavelength range.

Chapter 3: The Secret Of Intentionality

The preceding chapter, I addressed the fact that because you have a mind and your mind " modifies" what you see, you're constantly in charge. This is in contrast to what the majority of people perceive reality. We think that others have power, but we are not. The rich become richer and the poor are poorer. to make a slice of the pie to grow, the slice we share must be smaller. It is the case if we are living in a world that we did not create. We have to follow the laws that do not favor us.

This is the way that many people believe. In reality, we're all the time in control. It's easy for us to believe that we don't have control over our environment, and consequently, that we aren't in control of our own personal vibrations. It's why you keep hearing all kinds of excuses to justify these claims. I was born that way. That's how I am. I was the victim of a terrible incident and that shaped me for the remainder all my days. My ways are established. It's in my genetics.

It's my genetic destiny. I could continue on for hours. These are all lies. You know what the most damaging kind of lies are that we make up for ourselves. We deliberately tell ourselves lies because there is a reason why we would like to let go of our obligation to make any change we desires in our lives. It's far better to let the world change rather than us changing. Who would like this? It's a burden. It's a huge burden. It's better to think of yourself as a victim.

The victims aren't required to make changes. They aren't accountable since they're victims. Haven't they been through enough? I feel sorry for them. I know that sounds depressing and pathetic, but this is what people think. What do I know? Take a look at how they behave. If you'd like your life to be transformed then you must realize that you're in charge of the switch. You can alter the frequency sent out the vibrations that you receive them from the universe simply by shifting the knob of control or setting it to the desired frequency.

You can do it. You are the only one who can. I don't care about how many people tell them that they love your, or that you're perfect for them. They've got problems or knobs to deal with. They're not there to help you. They may inspire or help you however, in the end, you'll be the one to decide. You'll have become the person who pulls the trigger.

You can alter the vibrations by making the choice to speak, to think , and to live life with full intention

Intentionality is more than just a matter of intent. As I said earlier that the world isn't concerned about your motives or intentions. There's no reason to bother. It only cares about the things you do. It's clear enough, isn't it? This is where intention comes into play. If you're intentional that you do not stop in what you're aiming to accomplish. It isn't enough to abdicate the responsibility of your everyday life. If I've intended to do only the best for myself, and I've done my best. Have a great time with that.

It's not going to get far. It is imperative to plan everything. You must develop a sense urgency to the point that you modify your the way you do things. Your actions must reflect your intention. That's how you impact your surroundings in small way. This is how it begins. It manifests in actions. After taking action, there is reaction. It has consequences. What can you do to improve your focus?

Make a decision. Choose with intention who you think you ought to be.

The majority of people aren't able taking the time to do this. It's true that they eagerly follow what their parents or models they have been given. Generation after generation, people believe that they am like this. My parents were this way. They believed in the same values. I was impacted by something that happened to me when I was just a kid and that's what I'm working with. My past defines me. If you look around and see that everyone has a particular variety of values. You can consider that everyone else does it. That's me.

This isn't intentional. Intentionality is about choosing the person you want to be. It is about taking on responsibility. This means taking ownership of every aspect that you live in. You must reevaluate your beliefs, the possibilities you possess, your motives in mind, your motives, and motives. Do I really want this for myself? If not, what other motives goals, motives that are possible, as well as values exist? Take a look, I compare this to shopping at the supermarket.

When you go to the market, you have lots of items in your shopping cart. The majority of the stuff is in your cart due to the items the items your parents placed in there. Others put things there. You have neighbors, those who were with as a child, and family members. They are the ones who you see on television every day on a daily basis. They're the people who you listen to music. There's plenty of things you can put in your cart. Once you've made the decision to alter your vibrational frequency through embracing intention. You put the cart down. You move towards the back of the cart, and choose one item at a. You take a moment to look at every item and think do I really need? Do I look like the person I want to be? Do I have a higher ideal? Do these represent what I'm supposed to be striving for? In this moment, you are pondering the person you are truly becoming you'd like to be.

There is only one life to live. Are you planning to be living the life of your parents? Are you planning to go away and obliviously reflect on the lives of the people in your life? This would be a waste of time. Do you think this is the just one person? You can deliberately pick off the items in your cart, then walk down the aisle to select up new items. This is the shopping experience of universal vibratory. Add new motives, ideas and goals, as well as potentials and even values into your shopping cart. Now comes the difficult part. Think like someone with the motivations, motives and motives, goals, and values that you've deliberately chosen. Your mental outlook must shift. Your wavelength setting needs to alter. This means that you send diverse signals into the universe. And when the universe replies to a signal, you process it differently. You are a standard mental image. You attempt to model yourself on the traits that the person you are modeling yourself after. The greatest thing about this is that it is the person you decide to be. This isn't something you stumbled across. It's not someone who was dropped in your lap.

It's the person you choose to be. This is the most shocking fact. It doesn't matter what kind of the abuse you've experienced and how much money you have in your bank or whether you have money whatsoever. What level of skill or lack of it isn't an issue in this. The foundations are being laid and the possibilities of the universe will begin to manifest from the foundation you've learned. This will be the plan you'll follow, and while it may be slow for some people who have less resources, but It is doable. How can I tell? There have been people who have done this before. Many of us grew up in poverty. Their families were poor, and they're in a echo chamber, where everyone said you're poor.

It is not a good idea to imagine that you'll somehow get rid of all this. That's who you are. It's your destiny. You'll be be born poor and be poor. There are always those who can break out of this. They believe they are capable of doing it since they are in the same mentality as everyone else and view reality in exactly the same way as everyone else? The answer is clear. If you view your reality in the same way as everyone else in the scenario, you will receive exactly the same results as everyone else in the same situation. They adjusted their vibration settings. Everyone could see the dirt as well as gold ore.

Everyone was aware of challenges they would rather stay away from. They were able to see opportunities. Not less than one of the most successful men of all time John d Rockefeller grew up with an understanding of a place. The father of his was fraud, lying, and fraud. But. John D. Rockefeller overcame from humble beginnings. Many others were raised with abusive families however, they were able to overcome it. Did they happen to be luckier or are they genetically abnormal? Could it be an accident of fate? It was not, it was deliberate. You have to choose who you think should be . Everything will follow out of that.

Visible to invisible: visualize your vibrations as visible waves

Once you've chosen most purposefully and carefully who you believe you ought to be, here's the most crucial step that will flow back. You'll take control and control your energy. Prior to this you're walking around emitting vibrations, and the universe responds to your vibrations and you think that this is the case. This is the most accurate information you can expect. Wrong. You'll now transmit your personal vibes to reflect the kind of person you'd like to become. What's the key to success?

You'll be very deliberate about it. You'll be so deliberate that the vibrations you feel you transmit can be imagined as actual waves. When you have finished reading this article I'd like you to shut your eyes and contemplate thoughts. Think of those thoughts as real waves emanating from your brain. Now, do that. I'll wait. In a couple of minutes Did you notice anything? You are at the center of everything. If you think, the idea originates in your mind and radiates out into the universe. It originates from somewhere.

It originates from the center, and the center is you. When you release the visible waves. They are accountable and quantifiable. You can trace this idea to all humanity. As you consider your work What is the resonance? Who is it that it hits? Which one is most likely to be able to bounce waves back? If you consider the people you have relationships with, whom is it affect? Are there any waves could return? Be aware of the waves that come back. Where are they? What do they affect you? Consider, prior to the time I was aware of all this and prior to reading this book what was my initial reaction? Perhaps, you feel your body in a panic and your boyfriend or girlfriend is present.

What is their normal response? That's because you were radio waves transmitting. That's the wavelength you transmitted. There could be many other waves, but you're only focusing into or a narrow band , and it can affect the way you feel. Then, before you know it, you're saying certain words and you're doing specific actions. The reason behind this is that, for the major part, we are able to stop with it. This is the way we think.

We all have a tendency to think in a certain way.

You may be surprised to learn that your way of thinking is only one possibility. There are many different methods of thinking. Don't make me believe that it's just the way you are. It's just an aspect of who you are You were created this way. No. we're not able to do this. The reason is because you don't have control of your thoughts.

It's like it's happening or is a part of your. No. It's just a reflection of your attitude and energy. We view our lives as something like a movie. We take what we obtain. We mistake reality for something somebody else did, but it's the responsibility of someone else. They've made the first decision and everything else is a matter of the mind of. We are convinced that there is no role to play in the world we live in. This is why it's no surprise that if this is the case, then according to our collective belief system, we accept smaller and less levels of accountability. This isn't happening in a empty space, and when you make yourself believe that you are not responsible or control over the situation and then have lost the ability to make changes.

It's no surprise that a large portion of us feel like we're not in control and are stuck and the situation will get more and more difficult. Imagine that as just a child you had huge potential. You could be whatever you wanted to be. However, here you are and a mental prison. The potential is now turned into disappointment and decay. What's what's the "magic glue" that holds it all together? It's the habitual way of thinking. It holds everything in place because when you're in a downward spiral you're empowering yourself. If you begin with the same mindset and then you take actions that reinforce the attitude. You believe that this is the reality.

It is important to know the human condition of all of us. When you decide to live by intention you are free from this mental apathy. Your reality wasn't made by anyone else, it was yours. You created it yourself. Whatever is afflicting you and impedes your progress and sags you You chose it. The good thing is that you can change into a completely new person. It's just a matter of choosing the person you want to be and when you've made your choice it will start to flow since now you're likely to emit various vibrations, and you're likely to send your brain to receive different frequency.

Chapter 4: Solo Versus Group Vibration

In the earlier chapters, I guided your through altering the frequency of your radio signal to the universe by yourself. Your attention is focused on the radio transmitter. The trick is to be mindful of the frequency you transmit.

The best method to achieve this is to always be focused on the person you would like to become. What values does the person you want to be? What would their priorities be? Then, and the list goes on. Your vibrations will reflect this.

In a matter of minutes you'll be impacted by your state of mind and the way you perceive the world. This can lead to you choosing an alternative path in the way you conduct your decisions. When you alter the way you conduct yourself and behave, you've changed the game.

Seriously. This is when things drastically improve when you don't change your behavior. This is very good and well. There is only so high as you want when it comes to solo endeavors.

There is a good chance that there's the thing as group vibrating. When you collaborate with the other team, you can reach the place you want to be earlier instead of later.

Break the chains of routine thinking by group vibration

Let's admit it. The reason you're having trouble and why you're taking this book up initially is because you believe that you have no control in your own life. There are certain things that aren't yours to change.

All of this can be traced back to your own vibration. If you've chosen the wrong wavelength the power you generate decreases and lower. You might have completely lost the entire concept of owning yourself.

You're fortunate to have another device you can use. The first step is to reset your computer, as mentioned previously in chapters. There is however another tool that you can utilize. It's not a replacement for solo vibration. Let's make that clear.

You must be accountable. You must be aware of your own vibrations. There is no way to go about it. Group vibrations, on their own, when used correctly, will help make individual vibrations more easily. Group vibrations can be used to free yourself from

Begin by modeling your model

The first thing you must understand is that you've chosen to be a specific kind of person. Remind yourself that"I choose to be this, this individual does this believe in this, this individual is a person who responds to the world in with this attitude.

Create an outline. Reread it until it becomes clear. After that proceed to another step.

It is the next thing to do: stop blame on others. Your life has turned out in the way it did due to your decision. There's no one else to be blamed. There's no excuse.

Yes, your parents might not have been able to provide you with the best childhood, but it's over. This is dead and put to rest. It's the past. You are accountable for the present.

Sure, a bully in the schoolyard caused you to feel inadequate was humiliating, scolded you and made you feel embarrassed. This could have damaged confidence in yourself and damaged your self-esteem.

It's dead and put to rest because it's the past. You are accountable for your present. What is the reason you continue to be a slave to your past? Why do you continue nurture the wounds that brought you back and held you back for this time?

You have so much affection to share. There is so much you can give the world. What is the reason you let your past take the best of you? Release the blame-finding since that's not the way to go. other people for the mishaps that occurred in your life the more power you grant them.

Consider it. If they are the cause of whatever issue you're having trouble with, who's the solution? In this theory, not you. They created the problem, and they're the ones to fix it. They're the ones you turn to for repairs.

What's wrong with that "solution"? It's actually not even a solution. They've gone on. They may have forgotten the harm they caused you. Many of these people are dead.

It's difficult enough to make changes in yourself. Do you think of trying to influence other people? Therefore, stop searching as the answer and blame them. Let go. Be accountable for your actions.

Once you have a picture of the person you wish to become, repeat to yourself in complete confidence that I made my choice in life and I chose to be unhappy and I had the choice of being angry I decided to be unhappy, and I choose to be unhappy.

From the moment on, I'll be focused on the fact that I have the ability to pick and, from now from now, I will pick something else.

It is the way to can get in the driving seat for your entire life. This is how you can alter the frequency settings in your life. In the past you were set to the same frequency. This is why your life went in the way it did.

Be explicit about your discontent. It is important to be clear about your feelings. Make it clear that you're unhappy.

Now that you've got a clear understanding of all the facets of emotions I asked, what do you plan to do? It's easy. Make the switch. No one is pointing a gun at your head , causing you to suffer. You're not inside a physical space

Imagine how your vibration impacts others

After you've identified the ideal model of the person you wish to be and are taking complete control of your life following step is become the owner of the message you transmit. Think about the way your thoughts manifest into the words you speak to others.

Find the cause and effect line beginning with your thoughts and ending with your words, to others' reaction and reactions. Be aware that everything is a result of your taking the responsibility. Make sure you are as focused as you can.

I have a close friend with a mother-in-law who constantly says the incorrect thing at the right moment. Her words often can be very hurtful to people, and she is known to do it all the time. It was a problem that used to get my friend's head.

When she switched her frequency channel and reconnected with her mother improved tremendously. She stopped believing she could control her mother and instead accepted that she is an extremely shrewd person. She also recognized that everyone has flaws.

She started to feel happy with her mom's mistakes. What effect do you think that a single turn of the dial on her relationship with her mother?

She can now say without hesitation and no ambiguity that she's her mom's favorite, and that she is her mom's the best friend.

She was accountable for how she handles her world's vibrations and feedback. How? She altered her response to her and also the sound she sends back. It was discovered the mother of her child was much less likely to make rude insults when the friend decided to react differently to her.

Instead of provoking and instead of demanding the other person always explain or justify the things they did instead of expressing anger she took an alternative approach. Now , they're two peas in one pod. They're inseparable. She has affection for her mother.

It is possible to boost the power of this process by imagining the impact your vibration has on others. You may be asking yourself: why should I bother? Why should I take my first step? It's an aspect of being responsible. This is a part of being an adult.

Let's admit it. In the end, it could be the fault of someone else. In reality, it could be the scenario however, here's the issue. Will we sit and wait until they have their actions in order? Do we plan to prevent ourselves from taking full control in the event that they recognize the error in their actions?

Have fun with it. As you can see, it's difficult to make changes for yourself. Can do you think of trying to influence others? Are you imagining trying to convince other people to make the same changes you could have made for yourself?

Accept responsibility. Start with the first step. I'm sure it's unfair. It's not pleasant, however, do it nevertheless. You owe it to yourself.

Look for only the vibrations that are responsible for your model

What's the real reason to this dial switch that I'm constantly talking about? What's the deal? What's the point of changing your wavelength reception to a specific area? The answer is simple: it boils down to seeing signals that can create the image you wish to be.

That is that, when the world sends back a variety of signals, which of them will consolidate, strengthen, affirm and confirm my ideal self-image and who I would like to be?

There's a myriad of possible answers, right? However, it should at the very least have two main facets. It should counter these two forces. Which tendencies should you focus on? You don't have to see only vibrations to assist you in overcoming your instinctual urge to fight or fight.

This is a very human thing. It's in our DNA. However, unfortunately we prefer taking the shortcut instead of fighting. It's not about physical fighting or punching someone in the face, or hitting somebody on the head.

But, what I'm talking about is when you've got a job before you, and the combat or flight response and the response: I don't want to bother with this. It will take considerable effort. So, I try to find an alternative to push the can further down the road.

No. You can take it out now. It's true that it's daunting. But, guess what? You will be able to improve your skills by doing this work now.

Don't procrastinate. Don't kick the bucket further down the road. Don't transfer the responsibility to another person. Don't give excuses. Get it done now. Face your fears straight in the face and take control of it now.

You might be smacked back. It could be more powerful than you imagine. What do you think? If you're knocked back by a defender, you're building an ability. The trick is getting back on track and ensuring that business is taken care of repeatedly.

Are you sure it will be successful the next time? It is possible that you will be hit again and again. However, every time you choose to climb again up you become more and better. According to what Friedrich Nietzsche said, at most, "Whatever doesn't kill you will make you stronger."

Look for only the vibrations that will lead the model. And you must eliminate the two tendencies that you have such as your inclination to fighting or flight and your second one of a tendency to coast. You must always push yourself to the limit. You need to always push further and higher.

This goes for your relationships with your family, your education, work as a professional, your business, across the entire board. Let yourself be confronted. Accept being pushed to push yourself and reach that next level , and then the one beyond that. This is how you attain life mastery.

Does this mean that you'll be a millionaire? Sure, but not necessarily.

This isn't the point. Do you want to be the same person you were before? Passive or helpless and feeling that there's nothing you can do to change your life? Are you likely to be the one who is the one who creates change within your own life?

Increase the frequency of your visits and make sure you repeat it regularly

If you get some recognition from outside This tells you that you're doing what is right. You are advancing towards that person you'd like to be. What is your next step at that moment? You don't just coast. You'll increase your frequency.

In the same way, you take more actions. You are more active with people. They will respond to that signal. You can use this to motivate you to do more.

Then, you begin in a spiral upwards. The fact is that we all are naturally inclined for bounce-back signals. This is known as reciprocity.

If you consider it, it is burned in our genes. Why? If we hadn't reciprocated kindness in exchange for kindness, or harm against harm, we'd have been dead quite a while ago. We would have exchanged harm in exchange for kindness, or kindness in exchange for harm. In either case, it can lead to premature death.

The tendency to be a bit different doesn't pass through generations across generations. Therefore, we've got the ability to reciprocate in our genes. Make use of this. Your customers will bounce off your messages with tangible effects.

Also, if you're nice to someone and they are kind, they will show kindness back to you. If you go above and beyond to help someone, they'll be more impressed with your character. Your reputation will be better. This could open up a lot of opportunities for your.

If you notice this, you should allow it to alter your perspective. It will alter your perception of you. Let it affect your self-esteem.

What happens when you concentrate upon the kind of person that you wish to be? How do you perform specific actions that reflect the character's beliefs, preferences and personal traits?

You begin to alter your perception of yourself. You believe you're capable of much more. You begin to see the world in a different way. There is no longer a need to be a hostile environment which is determined to snare you. There is no need to be unjust, unfair and just plain mean.

Chapter 5: Create Your Own "Vibration Repeater Chamber"

I would like to explain to you how social vibration was a common occurrence. But it doesn't. It's only possible following repeated efforts. Most of the time there are plenty of circumstances that are beyond your control, however you must seek these out. They could be a huge help in helping your individual effort to raise your vibrations.

There's plenty you can do to address the issue of intermittent social reverberation. You can take matters in your own hands. How? Begin by surrounded by people who have the same frequency. That is, you'll create an echo chamber.

This is a place of safety for those who have the same values or wish to change their lives also. They have the same struggles as you, and are also looking to implement similar solutions.

Make sure you encourage each other by sending the appropriate signals

They could be your acquaintances. They could be your relatives and coworkers. The most important thing is that you're all on the same page. You're aware of the need to make a change. You are aware of the need to make improvements in your life.

The key is being as precise as you can with the messages you communicate to one another. You'll inspire one another however, you'll also need hold each other accountable to accounts.

The worst thing you can do to your friend who's trying to make a better life for themselves or herself is to tell them: "Well, it's going to be fine. You're unwilling to do it or you slowed down or did the easy route. That's okay."

No. You're not doing this person a huge favor. In fact you're poisoning your mind. It's not acceptable. It's not okay. Make them accountable. Remind them that you've chosen as this particular person. This is your ideal you, isn't it? We are on the exact line? Good.

What are you doing that isn't performing to the standards? What are you doing to avoid taking actions that reflect the values, character, and goals? What is the reason why this isn't happening?

If you do this, you are holding them accountable. What do they say? They reply with a statement: "Okay. I'm adamant that you held me accountable I'm going to hold you accountable."

You can take this in a negative way. You might think, they're just trying to get to get revenge against you. They're just trying to push back.

It's not, but it's the most beneficial thing that can occur. If you've reminded them that this is what they should be doing accept the fact that they'll respond with, "Hey, this is the norm." They're aiding you.

You now know the standard you must hold yourself to since people are watching. It doesn't need to be a battle. It doesn't need to be a sport of one-upmanship. It's a crucial aspect of having people who have the same values and are striving to hold one another accountable.

If you're doing this correctly it will result in pushing one another to make improvements. Another scenario that could happen is when you allow others to slack off as it's not enough for you to move from nothing to one. Trust me. It's an amazing victory, but the ultimate final goal is 100.

They are constantly pushing you to make improvements. They tell them "Okay good job. You've made it to one. Let's move on to two or what happened to three, and so on and so on."

Make each other work harder to improve. When you do this be sure to do so in a way which reinforces one another's ideas. Also, always return on the character they wish to be.

If they criticize you or motivate you, they will refer to the person you would like to become. This way , you can hold each other accountable to the process of growth.

You're not justifying one another. There's no holding hands. It's a matter of pushing each other up. Yes, it's annoying. Sometimes, it may even be offensive.

Here's the trick. The more you're offended and the more stubborn you are to make changes. If someone is holding you to account, you shouldn't feel in a state of shock. It's an opportunity.

It's true it hurts. The words can be hurtful. Everyone hates being corrected, but they accept it. Send the correct signals to one another. The more often you perform this action, the stronger your signal becomes.

How can you tell if you're creating the right sound?

At the conclusion of the day, whether you're performing solo vibrations or social vibrations group vibrations How do you know that you're on the right track? It's very easy. Simple. You'll be able to see the results.

If everything is in your head and you feel relaxed when you consider certain concepts You're not doing it right. You need to see tangible outcomes. Positive feelings do not suffice.

They're never enough. If you have the best intentions and the right mental games that you're playing , or even the perfect daydreams but they're not enough. They need to be effective.

They're important. They're a part of the game to fill but in the end, you're seeking outcomes.

Are you earning more? Are you getting more respect? Are you going to the gym more often to see your body change in the same way? Are you more healthy?

Have your interactions become more satisfying positive, supportive, and enriching? Do you feel that you are a more generous and giving person, and others are benefitting?

I could continue to go on. It's all about the results. But what if you don't see results? You can easily reset and alter your frequency setting until you're able to see tangible results.

When it comes down to it it's all about outcomes. If you see certain results, increase your frequency over time until you see even better outcomes.

Chapter 6: Basic Rules

Does life have a predetermined plan? Our experiences may make us think so. We have seen people born into wealthy families as well as people who were born into poor families. A person could be blessed with many talents while one may be totally lacking. If we don't understand why things take place in the way that they are, then we conclude that it's destiny. It's all part of a grand design by God. Certain people are accustomed to the idea that life's events are set in stone and expect the most favorable outcome. For those who don't believe this There is a way out. We can choose to make choices and our actions are important. Karma is the result of our actions.

At school, we were taught about scientific laws that help explain the reasons why things behave as they do under certain conditions. We are aware that humans aren't able to randomly travel space due to gravity. If the physical aspects of our lives are controlled by universal forces that govern other aspects of life , such as appearance and the place of birth should be controlled by universal forces too. The force of Karma that arises from our actions that produces outcomes that determine the conditions that we live our lives.

Since karma isn't directly visible or quantifiable it is impossible to conduct repeated tests or gather data as the scientific research. Instead, we have to be able to rely on our intuition when studying the karma. It is well-known that our eyes is able to detect a specific range of the spectrum of light. Light with wavelengths too short or long are inaccessible for the human eye. However, these invisibly visible light beams are surrounded by us and impact the human body in ways that can be beneficial, detrimental or all. Therefore, even although we don't have the ability to discern karma, we can claim that the invisible force is there that have an impact directly on us.

Maybe the next generation of technology will enable engineers and scientists to discover particle atoms that are connected to the concept of karma. At present we have only the knowledge of how karma functions by studying historical books and lectures. There are a lot of theories about karma which have been discussed time and again. When we understand the fundamentals that we will be able to let go from the notion of a destiny, gain an increased feeling of responsibility for ourselves, and take actions which will be beneficial for the future.

Death and Rebirth

Many answers have been provided on what happens after death. There are those who believe that we have souls that travel to Heaven or Hell. Some suggest that there are a variety of different realms we can reincarnate in, and some even say that we merge with God. One possibility we could rule out is the idea that energy ceases in existence after dying. This notion is contrary to the fundamental law that states that energy isn't produced or destroyed. Energy simply changes between forms and this is consistent with other solutions provided.

Rebirth could seem like a philosophical concept however, we can attempt to comprehend it with simple concepts. We are all aware the formula chemical used to describe water's chemical formula is H2O. To understand the formula we will concentrate on the oxygen portion of water. When water becomes hot enough, oxygen and hydrogen atoms are separated. The oxygen atom could connect with an oxygen atom and form O2 which is the gas is inhaled. Another possibility is that the oxygen atom that bonds with iron metal and forming the rust. If the water form currently in use "dies," the oxygen could be revived as an atom of gas, rust or another water molecule based on the force of attraction with other elements.

We tend to think of death as a single occasion and believe that rebirth only happens after the actual event. However both rebirth and death are occurring constantly. Human bodies are comprised by trillions of cell. certain of them are able to divide while others aren't able to. Every day, billions of cells die and then replaced with new ones or break into smaller pieces. Small changes can lead to larger mental and physical changes that affect our behavior as we age. All we need is to pay careful attention to the whole picture.

Karma acts as the glue that holds death and rebirth. If we wish to go from A to B, it is essential to be organized. Start by sketching out the different routes we could use to get to the point B. Then, we choose the best route and start our journey. Along the way there may be detours and delays that hinder us from progressing. It is possible to lose track to arrive at a different place. It takes a lot of diligence and effort required to get to our destination. The entire route from one place to the next is determined by the karma of our lives.

Karma 101

Good actions produce good effects; bad actions produce bad effects. This is the premise that karma is based on. There are other aspects to be considered. We can't stop the karma of others. It's not possible to make good choices and then store good karma and invoke the good karma when circumstances are difficult. In addition, karma does not have a set schedule. The results can be immediate or even in the future. Unfortunate events can occur to those who are good because their good actions may not yield positive outcomes in this life. Third, similar actions could generate different amounts of karma based on the circumstance. It is not wise to attempt purchasing the karma. Giving the gift of thousands of dollars could have the same effect that giving away just one dollar. Fifth, both good and bad karma could be combined to create an overall result. Positive actions can help lessen or counteract the adverse effects of bad karma through the years. In the end, we cannot erase our karma. In the case of most debts to money and loans There are laws that permit us to eliminate the debts. However, karma isn't so easy. We reap the seeds we planted.

Identifying the Actions and Results

The actions can be classified into four categories: actions that result in good Karma, actions that generate bad Karma, actions that create mixed good and bad karma and actions that don't produce bad or good Karma. Certain actions that result in positive karma will have certain effects. Giving the things we have to give away creates the karma to make us wealthier. Sharing information with others creates Karma that makes us more intelligent. Being generous and generous will result in positive karma which will create a beautiful appearance. Protection of those who are less fortunate than us will create positive karma and improve our health. Negative actions can cause negative Karma and the specific results they have result in the opposite.

The concept of intention as the basis of karma is a key concept throughout this book. There are many murky scenarios where we are unable to determine whether our actions are beneficial or bad. We can only guess. Even with the most sincerely intended intention, the actions we take may not result in the desired results. Making sure that we avoid actions that result in negative consequences is more challenging which is why that's where we should focus most of our efforts. Before engaging in any questionable actions it is important to analyze the motive behind it. If we are planning to harm others, the resultant action will cause an enormous amount of negative Karma. If the intention isn't in causing harm then we need to examine three aspects that include sound, sight, and suspicion. Things that cause us to observe harm being caused to other people or hear harm happening to others, or have a suspicion of that harm is being caused to others could result in bad Karma. The harmful actions we could have avoided but didn't, will cause an amount of bad Karma. The actions that cause harm, even if they are not avoidable, result in a small amount of bad Karma. If you can meet the three requirements do not result in bad good karma.

The Different Types of Giving

Giving money to those in need and charities is a popular method of boosting good Karma. There are numerous variables in giving to be considered. One factor is the kind of gifts. We can offer cash, time, tangible objects, or intangible things. Also, we must consider the recipient of our present. If we gift a present to someone who doesn't require it, then we'll only earn only a small amount of goodwill. A crucial factor is the intention. Are we able to benefit from the donation? Additionally, other factors like the amount of the gift and the time frame should be considered in addition.

Kinds of Gifts

When we think of gifting money, it is usually on the top of the gift lists. The reason money is attractive is because it does not take a lot of effort, aside from the work to earn the money. Individuals and businesses also love receiving money since they can spend it on items they really require or want. In the end cash is an excellent present for both the giver as well as recipients.

Time is another precious resource that is easily given. The time spent volunteering to assist people in need will create positive bad karma. As an example, we can visit hospitals and spend time with patients in need of companionship. We could volunteer in a soup kitchen or teach children. If we're busy professionals or professionals, we could take the time to assist others in the workplace or help them learn skills that can enhance their work performance. Finding ways to donate our time can be a good idea for those who don't have cash to spare. There are many ways to turn our time into good karma.

If we're not able to afford both cash and time, we are able to make good choices in our heads. For instance, if you are watching tv and see a report about someone making donations to charity, we should be grateful for the person who donated and for the people who are helped by the donation. When we hear of people struggling and we hope their circumstances will improve. When we set out to create good intentions and expressing good intentions, we are actually giving ourselves. The results may not be immediately apparent however there will come the time to take action on our goals and create positive and positive karma.

Even after our death even after death, we are able to donate a valuable donation: our organs. Organ donation is an issue that is controversial in many different cultures. We should follow our beliefs to influence our choices on this subject. If we donate our organs we could save lives. The doctors could make use of our organs to assist patients in need. Organs that cannot be transplanted could be used for research. This could help medical professionals and scientists get more efficient in their work. The advantages associated with this donation will assist us tremendously in the coming stage in our quest.

Donations to Religious Organizations

We all believe that giving money to religious groups is beneficial to the community. This belief was largely because of the religious reverence of religious figures and the belief that God will bless us when we engage in charitable donations to religious organizations. Religious organizations are not able to disprove this notion and support it in a certain way. Services to protect or erase the past sins are offered for those who wish to seek these services. Therefore, we should be aware of how religious organisations are helping the society when we give donations. Are they using the funds to aid the less fortunate and in need? We must also be able to determine if they are providing truthful teachings to people or if their teachings are based on superstitions or blind trust.

Nowadays, we are seeing leaders asking their followers to make donations to help renovate structures or to support their families. People who have strong convictions and plenty of resources often contribute large sums of money to their faith. There are many extravagant structures being constructed around the globe. The new statues are becoming larger and bigger, or they are adorned with precious materials like precious stones and gold. Certain leaders are dressed in extravagant clothes and driving luxurious automobiles.

Beware of the fanciful claims made by religious leaders. We shouldn't believe those who claim they have the power to treat diseases or boost fortunes when we give them enough funds. Some say they have the ability to talk to God or summon gods to control their bodies. Spending money on those who practice religion does not bring rewards. Instead, we could have bad luck from our past lives through being swindled. We must compare donations to religious institutions with other options instead of giving out of desperation.

Gift Recipients

Each dollar of donation does not mean the same. The recipients of gifts play an essential part in the amount of good karma can be generated through donations. Are they interested in or require the present? For instance, we could anticipate receiving little goodwill if we donate damaged items to charities which do not have any need for them. In reality, we could put unnecessary stress on these charities by requiring them to store or discard the items.

The only thing that is not directly related to the needs of the recipient are the resources available to recipients. Giving money to those who have lower resources is more beneficial than giving to those with more resources. It is possible to donate money to reputable, well-known charities with many donations. In addition we can donate our funds to hospitals and orphanages in countries with poor populations which are in need of funds. Money is more effective in less developed countries than wealthier ones.

Before making any donation, we must be sure to do our due diligence about the beneficiaries. Find out how they are spending the funds and whether or not they are honest about their intentions. This can be a challenge even when we attempt to apply the sound, sight as well as suspicion rules. For instance, giving money to someone who is homeless on the streets will result in good luck. If we suspect that the person is using the money for drugs or drink, then the amount of karma that we get will be less. If the homeless person makes use of the money to purchase clothing or food items or clothing, then we'll receive more good karma for the money we give them.

The recipients of gifts don't need to be human , either. It is also possible to give gifts to animals. The adoption or purchase of an animal is one method to aid. To get the most benefit it is recommended to choose pets who aren't wanted by others or are in danger of dying. The most ugly or old animal in shelters are great candidates to adopt. If adoption isn't an option, you can purchase a smaller animal like a fish or Hamster from the pet store and give them the best environment to reside in.

In some countries, the release of animals is often viewed as a means to create positive luck. This is the case if you release animals in a proper manner. You can visit the restaurant, purchase an animal, then release it into a freshwater lake. Are we able to gain any good luck from this particular act? It is likely that we have a little bad karma due to the fact that although our intentions were right we let the lobster go into hostile environments. The proper way to release the animal is to return returning it to the original habitat. In addition, we shouldn't release animals into unfamiliar environments when we are concerned that they may cause harm to wildlife in the local area.

Arguments for Giving

Why do we make donations? This question is the basis for determining the amount of goodwill we can earn through our charitable contributions. We may give to organizations that promote political causes or the schools we attended when we graduated. These kinds of donations do not generate much goodwill because these organizations are restricted in their tasks in the sense of aiding people who are in need. We should look for organizations that help human rights causes.

If we are looking for charities to support in, we must conduct studies on how the money donated is used by these organisations. Some organizations make use of funds in a wasteful way. They invest a lot of money on staff and advertising , instead of delivering actual results. These organizations should not be a part of. In addition, people from richer nations should consider charities in less developed countries due to differences in the purchasing power.

People give money to charities to gain the sake of fame or for personal gain. The charitable donations are a way to reduce taxes in some countries. If tax savings are the primary objective, the amount of goodwill received will be low. The same is true when gifts are intended to gain fame or appreciation from other people. If we consider it the good luck is being fulfilled immediately in the form of tax deductions or acknowledgement. However, these are small rewards for our good deeds.

We all know about Karma, don't be thinking of giving money as a means to purchase karma. If you try to purchase good karma is likely to reduce any good fortune earned. If we make a donation you want to do so anonymously. We should also not reveal the amount to anyone. For those who have enough, don't try to gain any benefit from the contributions. This means that you should not use the donation for tax deductions, or receiving the awards for generosity. Don't be concerned about receiving any reward for the donations. In reality, the most effective way to increase the goodwill earned from giving is to not thinking about it for as long as you can.

Foods that contain meat and vegetables

The transition from infanthood through adulthood demands us to consume a lot of food. It's a fact. it. But the different cultures have their own views on what constitutes the proper diet. Certain countries consider it acceptable to eat specific animals, whereas other nations are averse to the idea. Some countries place more emphasis on morality rather than taste or variety. These differences can result in discussions about what is the right and incorrect methods of eating.

Surprisingly, the diet may appear to have the potential for karmic consequences. If we are meat-eaters animal species, then animals must be killed to supply the food we need. If we're vegetarians then we're not going to witness animals being hurt because of our consumption. It is logical to think that people who eat meat have worse karma while vegetarians have better bad karma. It's not true whatsoever. Indeed, our eating habits result in neither good nor bad Karma after we have fulfilled the sound, sight, and suspicion standards.

Consuming Meat

The three requirements for eating meat that do not have bad karma is that you don't see the animal being killed, not hearing about the animal being killed or even imagining whether the creature was slaughtered in exchange for our dinner. As an example, we go to the restaurant and ask for lobster. If we witness the chef pull an entire lobster from the tank, and then return it to his kitchen that lobster dinner will cause us a certain amount of bad luck. If we order lobster but do not see or suspect that there are any live lobsters in the area the restaurant, then we're safe. To alter the scenario slightly, we went into an eatery and ordered chicken. There are no chickens in the wild, but we can hear the sound of chickens inside the restaurant. Our chicken dinner is not sound enough to meet the requirement.

The suspicion criteria can be quite complex. Although we may not see and hear an animal being killed, we could still suffer bad karma if animals are prepared specially for us. In the same way as the chicken story, imagine we're going to visit a friend whom we know is an agriculturalist. When we arrive at the friend's home and discover that he had prepared dinner for us using some of his chickens. In this instance we'd be sharing the bad luck that comes with the demise of this chicken. Because we didn't be aware of the dinner prior to time, we'd be able to be able to incur a small amount of bad karma since this chicken's demise was inevitable. But if we made a call ahead and our friend said they were cooking chicken in the kitchen, then the negative karma that we would have incurred could be more severe because we could have opted to not attend the food.

For people who enjoy meat The best method to avoid negative karma is visit a supermarket where the meat has already been prepared and packaged. Because the packages are put open for purchase by the public purchased, they're not restricted to a particular individual. Anyone can purchase meat packages without fearing negative karmic consequences. If we were to choose between vendors who treat animals in a humane manner versus sellers who do not treat animals humanely Which one do we select? The decision is based on what you're most at ease with. The meat from humane sources could have a higher price, and it's a luxury many people can't afford. But, selecting the humane vendors is better than those who are not humane because we strive to have positive ideas and goals always.

Vegetarianism

It is an excellent option. However, as we'll see at the beginning in this section, a healthy diet has nothing to deal with the impact of karma. Animals continue to be taken care of and slaughtered to make meat since the demand for meat will be constant for the foreseeable future. A lot of animals die due to the food we consume. The plants are regularly treated with chemical sprays to avoid insects from destroying them, and the chemicals they use can also contaminate the environment, causing harm to animals in the area. The decision is to choose an eating plan that causes the most harm, instead of doing none at all.

To elaborate on this issue to further explore this issue, let us consider the possibility that diet can affect the karma of a person. If this is true then, animals who eat only plants are likely to have a lot of positive Karma. Animals who eat other animals would have huge quantities of bad Karma. In this way, animals such as cows ought to have very joyful lives. However, this isn't the case because cattle are killed every day. Aside from dietary practices, other factors should be taking place regarding the Karma.

So , why should we bother becoming vegetarian? to strengthen positive thoughts in the mind through showing compassion to other creatures living on the planet. Mind is a bedding. Positive intentions can make soil fertile. A healthier soil will produce healthier plants , with more flowers and fruits. If you are able to do this it is possible to create more positive karma later on will increase. Vegetarianism can help increase this potential.

Karma-Friendly Diets

Based on the current circumstances like work and family being a vegetarian can be difficult.

There are numerous options to begin this path without completely into. If we consider our entire diet and lifestyle, we can gradually shift away from eating animals with four legs like cows to eating just two-legged animals like chicken to consuming exclusively aquatic animals. If we are a fan of a wide range of meats, you can consider becoming vegetarian for a portion of the time. For a start, we should eat only one vegetarian meal a week, which means three vegetarian meals in the time of a month be a full day of vegetarianism. Eggs, for instance, and milk are okay in the vegetarian diet. In fact, cutting down on the amount of animal species that we consume or restricting our consumption of meat is an impressive feat in itself.

Making changes to your diet could be challenging and shouldn't be done in a hurry. You should do some investigation before undertaking anything significant. If the new diet program begins to negatively impact our health or routine functions, we need to be aware and seek out alternative ways to improve ourselves. There are numerous ways to establish good goals. Dietary habits are just one aspect that could or might not be considered to be a part of the picture. In the near future the advancement of lab meat could resolve a number of moral dilemmas. If meat from labs is able to be produced without harming animals it could be considered an element of a vegetarian diet. In the end, we'll discover ways to eat our food that is more wholesome for animals.

Chapter 7: Different Types Of Theft

The karmic perspective is different from being a criminal in the context of societal rules. You may be walking along and spot a dime in the dirt; we take it and claim it as ours. The one who lost that money could be forced to accept the loss since police officers will not take the time to investigate such a tiny amount. In a an karmic sense, we've suffered some bad luck by taking that money that belongs to us.

Tangible Theft

The concept of tangible theft involves taking tangible items belonging to other people. This could range from a small pencils to larger objects like a vehicle. The amount of bad luck generated is based on the worth of the product of the initial owners as well as our motive for acquiring the object. The common sense tells us that taking cars will cause more bad karma that stealing the pencil. It is easy to determine out the quantity of negative luck if it was calculated solely on its price. However, the value of the product could be greater than the value in money.

We can make use of different sources like the internet or appraisals by professionals to assess the value for an object. However, this alone is not enough to assess the damages done to the original owners. Imagine that we rescued an item of jewelry from the ground. It is possible to determine a value for the item however, that price could be insufficient. If the object was an ancestral family heirloom or gift from a significant person or a significant other, then its value will be much greater than the amount of money. In this instance it is likely that taking these items will be a cause for us to suffer an increased amount of bad luck because the owner will suffer more by losing the item.

Even more the item could be more valuable to certain owners than others. It is possible to pick a dollar from the ground and believe that someone has lost a dime. However, the dollar will be more valuable for an owner who is not working than the owner who is wealthy. In this instance the negative karma will differ depending on the person who was the owner of the dollar. Because the calculations for karmic karma involve numerous unknown variables, even minor things can cause lots of bad Karma for us in the future down the.

Intangible Theft

The same rules are applicable to non-physical things such as music, art and ideas. This kind of theft has become more frequent today because of technological advances. It is easy to overlook that we are taking something since we do not have physically contact with the objects. Particularly, we may copy work from another and make it our own and then use it to benefit ourselves. In general, we can stream a film online or read a book on the internet or download software for free. costing.

Amount of negative karma that is created is contingent on the harm done to the original creator of the piece. A film, book or even software could come from a myriad of creators that range from big corporations to ordinary individuals. Therefore, we cause more negative karma to ourselves if we download something from a freelancer. The work they steal will hurt their financial wellbeing more because they are able to use fewer resources. Working with large companies results in less of negative karma since they have greater resources available.

Intentions to commit fraud

For years clever individuals crafted schemes to trick people into releasing money or personal details. There are laws to punish those who commit fraud, however law enforcement agencies are more likely to be attentive to cases that involve large sums of money or a large numbers of victims. Many criminals employ technology to create fake websites and emails to gather data from innocent users. We also hear of instances where people are lured into joining an illegal pyramid scheme. Anyone who is involved in these kinds of schemes are likely to suffer bad luck. This amount dependent on the extent of bodily or financial harm that others suffer because they did not know about the scheme.

Small-scale frauds can be very regular. For instance, we might attempt to sell defective products on the internet by making exaggerated claims regarding the product. We may feel that we are intelligent if the sale is successful through. But when looking considering the karma angle such actions are not recommended for a variety of reasons. The first is that it is a false speech. Furthermore, it is a type of theft as it's not an honest and fair trade. We will receive something of greater value than the other side. How much bad luck is contingent on the disparity in the price of the product as well as whether the buyer suffered harm by the product.

The reasons to steal

Motives behind stealing must be taken into account when calculating the amount of bad karma created. You can commit theft intentionally or accidentally. For instance, we want some pen at work to take notes, so we pick the first pen that we see and then never return it to its initial location. In this case there is no bad luck that is created is minimal because there was no intent to get the item. In contrast, when we search for a pen we choose to buy the one that is the most attractive. It is likely that the amount of negative karma generated is greater in the case of the second. In both cases, the quantity of bad luck that is created is not significant in both scenarios since we are able to see no harm to the owner as a result of the loss.

Many types of intentional theft can result in bad karma. However, the amount of negative karma that is created could decrease with the proper reason. If someone is in need and doesn't have the means to earn money, the person may have to take on a job to make ends meet. This is common in less developed nations. In the event of such acts, the bad karma is reduced and may even be realized when the perpetrator is found guilty. A person who is able to earn money and work but decides to steal will accumulate a significant amount of bad good karma.

In rare instances, intentional theft may result in both the bad and good karma. more good karma generated than bad. This is usually the case when the person who steals the items uses the stolen goods to better the society. The most common scenario is taking money from a corrupt businessperson or politician, and distributing it to the needy. However, even thefts that are motivated by good intentions can result in negative consequences. The person who steals could have to endure the consequences of death or jail before getting the benefits of good Karma.

Even with all the best intentions, it's best to stay clear of stealing completely.

The Different Types of Killing

There are two kinds of killing: unintentional and intentional. We could live our lives and try to prevent the killing of other living creatures, but it's challenging if not impossible. Unfortunate events happen and are out of our control. However, intentional killing is in our control, however. We must try to stay clear of intentional killing since the karmic consequences could be devastating. The intention is crucial when it comes to killing. In the absence of intention in the killing, the amount of negative karma that was created is minimal. If there was a motive, there is a lot of negative karma that is created can vary from moderate to huge.

Intentional killing

Intentional killing happens when we face the dilemma of whether or how to take the life of another. It is possible to plan in our heads or act on an emergency. For instance insects are usually killed without much consideration. If an insect bites us it is common to react and strike it with our fingers. If we notice ants moving around, we either spray the ants with chemicals or step onto them. There are instances where we could have decided not to carry out the plan, but did not. Intentional acts can result in some bad Karma.

The quantity of bad karma resulting by killing is contingent on a variety of variables. One of the main elements is the intellect and potential for further levels of education for the beings. A lot of bad karma is generated by killing creatures with greater capability to learn or intelligence. According to this logic killing an individual human being can bring many negative karma, since humans are thought to be the most intelligent animal living on earth.

Intelligence as a criterion is a difficult thing to measure. It is easy to recognize the distinction between killing a person and taking out an animal. However, the distinction between killing a person and killing another human being can be difficult to define. On a lesser scale killing ants could result in less negative karma than killing cattle or pigs. But, is it more harmful to kill a pig than goat? The answer isn't clear in this particular instance.

Another thing to be thinking about is the amount. It's common sense to say to say that killing dogs is less painful than killing an Cockroach. What happens to the quantity of bad luck when we attempt to balance killing dogs against killing a thousand insects. At some point, the amount of cockroaches killed in a row, for example one or ten thousand can cause more negative Karma than just killing one dog. It's the responsibility of the person to decide the acceptable level of cockroaches.

Fishing and Hunting

Hunting for enjoyment as a sport or to help with controlling population growth is accepted as normal actions. There are no laws that prohibit humans from killing wild animals. But, killing animals to satisfy our natural urges or to show something to ourselves is likely to only result in negative Karma. If we are not in a dire situation, where we were forced the need to fish or hunt for food, there's an excuse not for killing animals from a spiritual viewpoint. Therefore, fishing and hunting is not a good idea. We can earn money to purchase food items.

It is possible to argue that animals fight each other constantly. The tigers and the lions consume lots of meat. Goats and cows consume lots of grass. Do tigers and lions have lots of bad karma as compared to goats and cows due to their diets? The problem here is that it boils to the level of intelligence. Animals aren't able to know more. The tigers, the lions, cows goats, and other animals do not differentiate between food that is good as well as what's bad. They are just hungry to them. Humans are more intelligent than any other species on the planet. We must use our intellect to cultivate empathy for the other species and not profit from their intelligence.

Intentional killing

The unintentional killing of another can happen in a way that is completely unnoticed by us. Every living thing can live without killing another living thing. For instance, in humans many microorganisms and bacteria have been born, then destroyed each second. In a larger sense insects are killed as we walk, ride our bicycles or drive our cars. We are a an integral part of the cycle of death and life for many species during our everyday routine.

What are the karmic repercussions of accidental killing? To solve this issue we must be able to distinguish between bad karma from the past and the new bad Karma. For instance, we're driving and struck another motorist crossing the road. The bad karma we have from our previous experiences is the reason for the incident. A new quantity of bad karma is created as we see damage caused. This amount that is created will be minimal for accidental murder because there was no way to have prevented the killing. There is a high possibility that we will suffer the consequences of our new bad karma that we have created in this life. In the above scenario, we may be subject to fines and prison time following the incident. If we take a different approach in which we attack a dog in place of a person. In this case, we do not face any legal penalties, however the new bad karma could make us feel anxiety and depression that we need to get over. When we've were punished both the old and the new bad karma is solved.

Although acts of accidental killings can happen at any moment however, we have the responsibility to stay clear of dangerous situations. For instance, we must not drink alcohol if there is a possibility that we are required to operate an automobile. It is not advisable to use any drugs that can cause us to lose control and engage in acts of violent or theft. By observing laws and refraining from engaging in illegal things can save us from pain. If we continue putting ourselves in controlled circumstances and make good choices and do not commit any unintentional sins, the bad karma resulting actions will be nothing more than minor inconveniences.

Suicide

It is important to think about a specific type of murder that is deliberate: suicide. Anyone who is considering suicide should never go through the process. It is a decision that can result in a lot of negative luck. It is believed that those who commit suicide are likely to end up in a different situation after their dying than the situation they are at the moment. The people who commit suicide tend to do so in order to avoid bad karma that they have suffered in the past. However, there is no escape from the karma of others.

We are aware that killing a human causes a significant amount of bad Karma. There's a range that determines the severity of the bad luck that is created. The act of killing a stranger is not good and killing the close family member or friend is more serious; and committing suicide is among the most harmful acts one is able to commit since it results in quite a lot of negative good karma. It is also not recommended to commit suicide with assisted suicide. All pain and suffering that ends during this lifetime could be carried into another life if bad karma remains unresolved. Additionally, assisted suicide could be unlawful and medical professionals could get into trouble for conducting the procedure.

There are some exemptions from the rule of suicide. One of them involves intelligent people and women with an understanding of the what is going on in the world. Another example is when suicide was committed in order to ensure the safety of other people. We have seen numerous instances in the past of generals who sacrificed their lives to protect their troops or captains who went down with their ships to make space for other lifeboats. Sometimes we hear of someone who commits suicide in order in protest to something. It's a murky zone because it's hard to tell if the person is truly intelligent or simply stubborn. The main issue is that suicides do not always result in the necessary modifications.

Anyone who is seriously thinking of taking a suicide risk should attempt to get help. If we have a choice which one to make, we should decide to live our lives. We should be more helpful to people by living, working and contributing to the society. We must be able to confront old bad karma today instead of avoiding it. It is important to continue to face the challenges that we face and do acts of kindness every time we have the opportunity.

Abortion

Another instance of intentional aborting is an abortion. The standard rule is to not have an abortion in normal situations. If a woman doesn't make use of birth control and becomes pregnant, it would not be an appropriate reason to dispose of the child. In the event that the child is not wanted because of financial limitations or the responsibility of being a parent is too much, placing the baby to adoption could be an alternative. If not, then the father and mother will have to work together to raise the child. It could be a battle but the mother could consider it as solving old bad karma.

Some exceptions where abortion is permitted include the risk that is posed to the mother or if the baby has defects at birth that may hinder the normal development of. If the mother is likely to die during the birthing process and the baby is born with defects, then a case can be made for aborting the baby. The adult's life is worth more than the baby's life. Problems must be discussed with doctor prior to making a decision on an abortion. If an abortion is thought to be impossible, just a small amount of bad karma may result from performing the procedure. The bad karma caused by the procedure could appear immediately with the appearance of emotional pain and suffering.

The situation where a baby may be born with deformities or imperfections is a challenge from a karmic point of view. Mothers can deliver the baby and then try to nurture it as well as they can. It is a lot of bad karma due to previous misdeeds. The family could resolve the issue now or put off the issue through an abortion. However, the decision is difficult and should be considered with care. If you decide to have an abortion it is best carried out early in order to reduce the chance of having bad luck. The more mature the baby becomes and it is the worse karma produced. Err to the right side of caution whenever possible.

The reasons why killing is necessary

There are numerous legitimate motives to kill. You can take on the job to provide food or protect ourselves This is acceptable in the event that we find ourselves in a situation that is incredibly difficult. However, if we have enough funds to buy groceries for ourselves, then we ought to buy food, not kill to get it. In addition, if something poses an imminent threat to our family or us it is best to explore every other option before using violence. The amount of negative the karma that's created will be small since the primary concern is to protect ourselves and others.

Cops are entitled to take down criminals who can cause harm to other people without worrying about negative good karma. They would have gained good karma, if the victims are saved. It is important to remember that violence should not be the final recourse. If the criminal surrendered and were killed by cops, then it was a different story. Police killing innocents because of miscommunications could result in bad good karma. The severity of the bad karma will depend on whether the incident was possible to avoid or not.

Involuntary killing is more risky. Insanity, jealousy and greed could cause actions that result in an abundance of negative good karma. Over-indulging in money or love is often the case. Negative thoughts cause specks of negative karma within the mind. The mind eventually is full of negative seedlings of karmic karma that are waiting to be given the proper moment to germinate. We must get rid of negative ideas by filling our minds with love and compassion of others, even those we don't agree with. Then, the negative potential of our karmic life begin to fade away and better circumstances will begin to establish themselves.

Relationships

It is believed that the people whom we meet are already connected to us from past lives. In the past we had parents and children, loved ones or friends and enemies. Based on the way we treated other people throughout our lives they could be reunited again in a state of joy or sorrow. The people we once admired could become our current adversaries; on the other hand the people we once fought may be current acquaintances.

As we aren't able to remember our actions in the past We should treat people in our relationships today with respect. We should be considerate in our thinking, actions and words when we're with others. Each relationship is only short-lived. One of the most important goals in life is to lessen our karmic ties with others to ensure that we don't end in a never-ending love-hate loop.

Parents

One of the strongest bonds that we have to be a part of our daily lives lies our parents. They supported us and cared for us in times when we were not able to take care of ourselves. We owe them our most sincere gratitude. For this reason, caring and generous actions towards our parents can bring about an abundance of positive luck. Parents can cause anger for us. However, we must take the time to put our frustrations aside and look after our parents whenever they require it.

There are times when parents take their children away to be cared for by another person. They were absent or died. Children should treat the people who raised them as biological parents. Additionally, children should not be bitter towards biological parents who have moved away. In reality, they must find ways to assist their biological parents as well as to adoptive parents in order to create positive karma.

As parents age their capacity to perform regular activities may be reduced. It is important to be able to take care of them as they did ourselves when we were children. Accept all the shortcomings they may have as they age. In doing this we're not only aiding them but aiding ourselves too.

Friends and Family

Certain relatives and friends are beneficial while others make us go down a wrong path. It is crucial for us to recognize those people and relatives who are helpful as well as those and relatives that can be harmful. In particular, we need to be wary of relatives and friends who are encouraging us to engage in drugs or engage in criminal activity. Instead it is better to hang out with family and friends who are kind and caring. Place ourselves in difficult situations by locating the appropriate people. If family members and friends are in trouble We must try to help them by providing them with the needed support.

Certain relatives and friends share deep karmic bonds We will stay close to them throughout the course of our lives. In relationships where the bonds are less strong the paths may diverge over time. Our closest family members, brothers, or sisters might share our interests when were younger. As we grow older, they might be interested in things that we aren't keen on. There are disputes and disagreements with each others; jealousy and envy can arise when we become mature. Conflicts can lead to further problematic karmic situations. We can attempt to fix relationships, but in the end, the best option is to leave the relationship.

Marriage Partners

If we meet that one we love we'd like to ask the person to marry us, and then become part of the family. There are many kinds of marriage like monogamy, polygamy or married by arrangement, and the similar-sex marriage. These marriages do not produce negative karma if the both parties have given their full consent to be part of the union. The use of force or tricks should not be used to convince someone to sign a marriage contract.

After the marriage has been completed and the couple is married, the future of their relationship will depend on the karmic bond between us and our spouses. It is possible to live the remainder of our days together or split up in the midst of months. There are many things that we can manage to lessen the likelihood of a breakup for example, not being enticed to engage in sexual adultery, verbally or physically assault our partners or even physically abuse them.

The negative emotions of anger and jealousy should be prevented. For instance, if we earn more than our coworkers and we are able to be able to use our success to influence them or scold them when they do not listen to us. However when we're the ones who earn less then we shouldn't be irritated by the fact that we are making less money. Instead we should be content that our partners share their success with us and we should help the other ways they are able to help.

Marriages can break down due to events outside our control. The partners could be cheating on us or develop a health issue or even have changed their minds. A relationship that has ended or are on the verge of ending can be troubling. There is a feeling of sadness and alone as we lose our loved ones due to illness or accidents; or we might feel angry and resentful when our partner requests to divorce or split. This is bad past karma coming to come to. Its resolution could cause spiritual bonds we have with our companions to break. As passengers on a ship individuals must depart when they reach their destination.

The actions of anger or hatred towards our loved ones could lead us to be reunited as adversaries. On the other hand there are those who love their partner so much that they want to have them back. This is not a good idea because although we might encounter our love in another moment, there's no way of knowing the conditions under the relationship we share. We could live a blissful life, or experience terrible circumstances with each other. While we don't know our past actions it is best to just enjoy the time we spend with our loved ones and then leave the relationship when it is appropriate. You can't ask for more.

Children

When we have children we must provide food, clothing, shelter and provide financial aid for them until they're old enough to care for themselves. Some children become well-off and go off to go off on their own. Some children may need parents' support for a lengthy period of. Parents with good karma could witness their children achieve and remain around in later their lives. People with poor karma could have their children struggling.

If the child is being scheduled and/or not we need to make sure that we take care of the child in a proper manner. The consequences of abandoning our child could be for them to grow up in a dysfunctional family and cause irreparable harm. It will also create a lot of negative Karma. Parents who decide to leave may have to provide child support, and may lose the chance to be able to reconcile to their kids in the near future. Therefore, the choice of bringing the child into the world is an important one that requires careful consideration by parents as well as the child's parents.

Additionally, through adoption or marriage, we could have children who aren't biologically ours. The best way to handle such situations is to treat the children as our children. Even if we adopt biological children in the future, we shouldn't pay less focus on our adopted children. They're no different than those born to us from a spiritual perspective.

We can use a variety of methods to assist our parents, friends family members, children, and relatives have a fulfilling and happy life. One of the most effective ways to aid one person is to expose them to the right and wrong behaviors. Explain the concept of karma to them and educate them on ways to produce positive results in the near future. If, for instance, we witness our children engaging in a game of killing bugs and have them kill bugs, we must gently remind that they should stop. Parents can suggest they donate to charities or stop the negative habits they've learned throughout their lives.

In sharing our expertise by sharing our knowledge with others, we will aid them in their preparation for the journey ahead. Karmic makeup is similar to an item is carried from one place to another location. Understanding karma can help us to get rid of unnecessary baggage and bring in additional essential items to aid us in our travels. Even if people who are near us do not believe in karma, having the basics of what's good and bad is extremely useful. When the right time comes to do so, they'll look up the subject on their own.

Different types of careers

Food shelter, clothing, and food are all essential to our daily lives. The concept of money long ago to make trading easier for various parties. We also have a system that we can use in order to make money. Businesses are created to market goods and services. Another option is to work to private and public institutions. In the majority of cases the work we do has little negative karmic consequences. However there are some dangers to look out for while working.

Certain occupations offer us the opportunity to help or harm other people. The amount of karma we can generate in these jobs is contingent upon the amount of benefit we bring to others or the harm we cause and the quantity of living creatures that are affected. Another crucial aspect to consider is the long-term consequences of our choices. Therefore, we could be required to confront karma that has been created through our work, even if we have left the position some time in the past.

People with a lot of good luck accumulated through previous lives might end up in top positions on their path to success. They could be anywhere from a managers to kings or president of a whole nation. If we happen to hold one of these positions, we'd be able to issue orders to the people below us, and take decisions that have a direct impact on the lives of many.

Presidents and Kings

The most highly coveted positions that only a handful of people be able to achieve is the position of head of the nation. Due to the development of many years of good karma, many became kings and queens in various points of the history of. It is still a thing but the majority of nations have changed their leadership roles to prime ministers, presidents or dictators. Karma is good and bad, but it's increased by leaders. Presidents can cause additional hardships for people by increasing taxes or cutting welfare benefits, thus generating an abundance of negative good karma. However, a president can reduce the bad karma making laws that lower taxes or create jobs or offer better benefits to those who are poor.

It may seem unfair to have dictators in charge of an entire nation for the bulk time. We must realize that they have an abundance of positive karma from their previous lives. They might have exhausted the majority of it through wronged things in their lives however, there's enough good karma left to let them live happily in the present. The bad karma could be observed for a handful of dictators who are deposed or imprisoned. Or even executed. For those who have lived their life without scratching it and have no regrets, their bad karma will be a problem in the future.

Managers and owners

It's very fortunate to get into the post as an owner of a business or a manager. While the decisions made by business leaders may not be as important as those taken by kings or presidents but they can be a major influence on the workforce and the communities they serve. Business owners go through fluctuations. Based on the business environment owners are able to either increase or decrease the number of employees and also cut or raise the amount of wages, relocate to new places, or implement new technologies.

There is a small amount of negative karma when you let people go in times of poor and the goal is keeping the company running. However, good karma may be earned by owners who try to retain employees during the tough times so that they don't end up being forced to work. It is more difficult when companies are in good health and the decision is made to make replacements to increase profit. Outsourcing is either positive or negative thing, based on the amount of employees affected by losing their jobs at the old location and how many employees benefit from in gaining new jobs.

What is the nature and character of an business is an additional factor to consider. If, for instance, we are in a field which produces harmful products, like drugs or weapons and promote them in a manner which encourages children to take the products, then we'd be able to suffer some bad Karma in relation to the harm caused. In contrast, if we were in charge of charitable organisations and choose to expand ways to aid people, then we'd receive a certain amount of good karma based on the benefits that are provided.

A variety of products can be harmful if manufactured using inferior components or used in a non-safe way. Owners and managers have the obligation to provide customers with clear information about the dangers of the use of these products. Business leaders who made the decision to utilize inferior components in order to save money, or to conceal dangerous information from their customers could be punished for their actions based on the number of customers affected and the extent of the damage. The bad karma may be realized immediately through lawsuits, dismissal or even imprisonment.

The hiring and training of employees are another way that managers and owners can earn positive karma. Employers with good employees can help their businesses grow, but hiring employees can be a bit subjective. Certain managers choose to hire family members or friends even though they're not the most ideal candidates. A good amount of karma is created when this happens. But hiring managers must be able to distinguish between applicants who want the job and those who require the job. If it's not too big of a problem, they should consider hiring people who have not worked for a prolonged period trying to make it into the field or are part of the group of people who are targeted for discrimination. They are more likely to be grateful to be given the opportunity and will result in positive karma for the hiring managers.

Once the hiring decisions have been taken, the proper training needs to be given to the employees in order to ensure they are successful on the job. Certain managers and owners could opt to cut costs by providing only limited instruction or even no training in the first place. Employees might be unable to perform their duties effectively, and leave the job or get fired. There's a small amount of negative karma for business owners due to the highest turnover of employees or have a bad reputation. A lot more bad karma is caused if the work involves dangers and the employee is injured in any way because of poor education.

For companies with great employees, it is difficult to let them decide to quit. Some employees will send a notice to leave within a couple of weeks. Some employees may quit without notice, causing disruption to the company. In any case, it's crucial for managers and owners not to get angry. The karmic bonds between employees are broken. Be a trustworthy reference for them in the event of need and wish them all the best for their next endeavors.

Scientists and Inventors

The people who create new products and services can be able to bring positive or negative karma based what the industry. For instance, if scientists are conducting research on new drugs within a pharmaceutical company then we may be able to earn good karma when we find medicines that aid people. The likelihood of getting good karma is higher in the event that our aim is to help people and not be purely profitable.

On contrary it is possible that we are testing products on animals, which may not bring much value for society. In this scenario it would create negative karma by hurting animals. Even if the product does offer benefits to other people, the any good karma that is created may not be sufficient because we weren't the initial inventors, but we are the ones directly responsible for killing the animals, and will be accountable for the bad karma created by the actions of these animals.

It is crucial to have a plan when it comes to inventing something. For instance, we might create a scientific discovery that could have a variety of uses. However, the way in which the findings are utilized could not be entirely under our control. The companies we work under could be the sole decision-maker in the way our discoveries are utilized and could result in the development of new substances or weapons. There is no chance of gaining positive karma if our discoveries are employed in negative ways. However, if our discoveries were employed to benefit society in the way we was intended, then we will receive some positive karma.

Laborers and Service Workers

The majority of jobs in the service and labor industries do not come with any serious adverse karmic implications. There are some risky work-related jobs to avoid. Some of them require the killing of animals like butchers, fishermen and exterminators. The work of these jobs can lead us to accumulate negative reputation over time. It is recommended that we seek out other opportunities which don't cause harm to other living creatures.

Trafficking in human beings and selling drugs are both dangerous jobs. Traffickers can directly harm others and are likely to receive a significant amount of negative luck. Drug dealers sell products that can lead to addiction and can be harmful for the buyers. Dealers could even be addicted to these drugs for themselves. This can create the cycle of bad karma being fulfilled as well as new bad karma being generated.

The people who create these kinds of jobs may suffer more negative karma than employees since they are the ones responsible for the hardships that are imposed on others. So, like employees, owners must find different businesses that can earn them an income if they can. If one isn't able to find a new job and is unable to find another, they should attempt to establish a repentant attitude for the harm done and strive to not return to the same activities in the future.

Different types of vices

The majority of living beings for the of us want to enjoy and stay away from discomfort.

We have a variety of ways to be content or forget about our troubles. We can drink, take drug, enjoy games and much more. These aren't in and of themselves. However, the problem arises when we begin spending more and more resources on these things. In time, we'll become dependent and are unable to pull ourselves away, even when negative signs begin to show up.

In this chapter, we'll explore a number of actions which can be harmful once addicts develop. The effects of addiction can be determined by the extent of harm that is caused to the addicts as well as those associated with them. In the case of addiction, we could be confronting bad karma from the past, while making new bad luck in the same while. Anyone who is suffering from addiction must seek out professional help.

Alcohol and drugs Alcohol

The proper use of alcohol and drugs is beneficial. Modern medicine can aid in managing the symptoms of illness and pain. In addition, drinking certain alcohol drinks in moderation is a beneficial. The effects of drinking and using drugs can produce only a small amount of good or bad luck so long as we're at the helm of our choices. We can also overestimate the power of our minds and body. If we drink too much and behave in ways that can't be thought to be normal.

If we begin physically or verbally abusing people around us, we can create bad good karma. The consequences can be swift as relationships damaged or laws break. There are many stories in the news concerning domestic violence divorces, arrests, and divorces in connection with addiction. For those who are addicted and can avoid social consequences, using drugs and alcohol can take a significant impact on their health and mental health. Use alcohol and drugs only according to the advice of health professionals and stay clear of excessive recreational consumption.

Sexual Activities

Sexual indulgence by a partner who is willing to share it with you or by pornography is completely acceptable. The problem is when we're trapped in a state of constant needing.

We are able to focus our thoughts, actions and even are obsessed with sexual pleasure, and we constantly search to the next experience or the more enjoyable experience. The people who try to achieve lasting happiness by sexual intimacy will always be unhappy and disappointed.

The risk of addiction is when we begin to view your sexual desire as tangible objects. The partners we choose to partner with become commodities for our pleasure. Addicts may engage in harmful behavior that range from sexual harassment sexual assault to adultery. Additionally, they are at a higher possibility of getting sexually transmitted illnesses. They'll be stuck in a pool of negative Karma in the near future.

A fascinating case of sexual activity is prostitution. If we offer money to an individual to get the services of sexual sex, then we may cause direct harm to the prostitute, as well as indirectly harm by encouraging trafficking in human beings. Even if the individual chose to be a prostitute of the decision and choice, we should not make use of this as a reason for our choice to pay for sexual services. If our motive is to assist prostitutes, there are alternatives available. From a spiritual point viewpoint, we should stay clear of sexual acts that have the potential to cause harm to our companions by talking about what is acceptable.

Gambling

Gambling is a common sport if we are able to manage the amount we invest. There is always a possibility for a substantial amount of bad or good luck to be realized when we gamble. We could become millionaires in one day or even lose all of our money. As the odds of losing significantly higher than the chance of winning, it is best not to gamble more than we are able to afford losing. If we are gambling often, then it is possible that we be suffering from an addiction issue and are in a vicious cycle of bad karma. This is the reason we should only gamble when we are able to manage our impulses.

A big win, especially one that is large amounts, can cause us to be anxious. We will surely be pestered by those asking for favors when the details are released. However, we are certain that we are not getting as bad luck now than prior to. Certain winners are able to stay in the game There are also instances when winners have to go through all their money and find themselves in tough times. They are entangled in their way of life and begin to develop bad habits that could cause them to be in prison or even die in certain cases. We can attempt to prevent unfortunate events by taking a portion of our gains and doing positive acts. It is like reinvesting our good luck to create more good positive karma.

Chapter 8: Types Of Speech

There are numerous ways we can communicate with others using the written word, spoken language as well as nonverbal messages. Speech can be used to entertain, instruct and persuade or even to inform. Based on the goal for the talk, it is the possibility of bringing good or bad luck. For instance, we could assist other people learn a crucial ability that they can apply in their the real world. This can be accomplished by an educational program, a book or even videos. If we intend to harm someone else, we could point out their shortcomings. We must avoid kinds of words that cause harm to other people and to ourselves.

Certain countries permit greater freedom of expression than other countries. Certain democratic governments are tolerant of and even encourage the expression of dissent. The freedom to speak freely is not a reason for us to utilize it in a degrading manner. We are accountable for our opinions and actions. It is essential to consider the subjects we choose to communicate to other people. This analysis should be conducted prior to and after the process of communication. If the harmful speech has been made before it is our responsibility to rectify the situation in the greatest extent of our abilities. It is a daunting task since we aren't able to make amends for what has been spoken. The best way to approach this is stopping at any time in the speech if you believe it will cause damage than good.

False Statement

False speech occurs when the information we provide is not backed up by real facts. That means we didn't look for evidence to back our assertions. When we encounter ideas we'd like to implement it is important to determine whether the ideas come coming from trustworthy sources. Do not believe the information we receive from those close to us like our family members or relatives. We must also exercise care when talking about personal experiences , because the information we have for ourselves may not be the case for another person.

There are instances when we have the facts and we do not embellish the facts in order to appear more convincing when we present our case. One example of this is when people appear in the courtroom. The prosecutor and defendants will give evidence that will make their opponents appear more threatening than they actually are. It could lead innocent people to be punished that they are not entitled to or cause guilty persons to avoid penalties. The party who loses of the argument could be hurt, which can lead to negative luck creating.

It is also important to think about timing when working with the speech. Certain facts are repeated many times. But, certain facts could be false in a matter of minutes. It is imperative to check whether the information we're giving are relevant to our target audience. For instance, we might think that we utilize 10% of the brain. It is now known that we utilize nearly every brain part. It would be confusing to people by continuing to tell people this story. It is not a good idea to let material from the past guide us to continue making false claims believed to be truthful.

Speech that is deceitful

What happens if we purchase something like a car , and the owner isn't aware of the actual value of the item however, we are aware of its actual value? It is possible to be honest and give the owner the right price , or offer an extremely low price and hope that the owner accepts the offer. From a realistic standpoint, it is prudent to seek to sell the item for a lesser cost than what is actually worth. You may even feel proud in proving someone else wrong. However, from spiritual perspective, deceit in any form must be avoided as it can cause negative Karma.

Why would this happen in the event that the seller does not have all the details? When we engage in this deceitful act we are consciously trying to swindle the seller. The seller may require money to cover urgent expenses Our actions may result in real harm to people who are struggling. The bad karma generated would depend on the extent of harm that is caused. If the person selling the money did not require the money, then just a tiny quantity of negative karma could result from our deceit. If we suspect that the money was intended for medical treatment or to settle debts in the first place, then real harm was caused and some bad karma could be caused. However, we shouldn't act in deceitful ways since we don't want other people being deceived by us too.

Idle Speech

We're committing idle talk when we are speaking to fill in the silence. It is possible to talk about topics like jokes, gossip and daily observations or material from the realm of fantasy. This kind of conversation is a great way to establish relationships between us and our fellows. It is, however, difficult to know how other people react to our incessant speech. An issue that is easy for us may create discomfort for others. This is the case when we talk about religion or politics. People come from many different environments and have different beliefs. We need to be cautious when we speak to someone isn't close to us.

One type of idle conversation that we must try to stay clear of is gossip and gossip. There's no reason to discuss someone behind his or her back. When we've got something positive or positive to share about someone we must tell them. If we say something negative about someone else, there will always be a chance the person will find out and become upset. Alongside gossip or making rumors about others could result in us breaking the false speech rule and also because the rumors could prove to false. If the rumors that surround an individual are false the person upon whom the rumors are based may find themselves in a negative environment. Even when the rumors are positive they could trigger an element of jealousy among the people who love the person.

When we feel close to an individual, we usually interact more easily with the person. However, people change over time. The subjects that were acceptable to discuss in the past may trigger negative emotions in the present. This is evident in couples who are married. Before we get married, we were able to discuss features we like about other people or prior relationships. However, talking about these same topics after we've been married may cause our partners to become annoyed or discussed in subsequent disagreements. A joke that is merely about the way someone appears or acts could be taken in a negative way. There's an appropriate and appropriate time for idle talk. If the timing isn't longer appropriate, silence is the best.

Harsh Speech

Speech that is violent could be the most damaging kind of speech when in comparison to other types of speech. On a wider scale, conflicts could be attributed to speeches delivered by politicians to promote their views against other nations, races or religions. On an individual level relationships can break down and violent acts may be committed against one another in extreme instances. We should be careful not to communicate in a manner that triggers negative emotions.

It is possible to avoid inappropriate speech by scrutinizing the language and tone of our spoken language. When speaking it is important to talk in a calm and respectful manner. Shouting is only appropriate those occasions where we need to inspire others or speaking to someone who is experiencing hearing difficulties. Additionally, the words we use in our speeches are important. Certain words are considered to be demeaning to other people and if used, could trigger intense reactions. The same is true for curse words. The words we curse are commonplace in our vocabulary, however, strangers whom we meet aren't aware of that. We might not even be aware of when our speech is causing distress to people around us.

When we use harsh language to intimidate or provoke anger by using harsh words, we are creating the base for negative karma to multiply. If our words cause people to hurt their own or others, we will be rewarded with a certain amount of negative Karma. For instance, a person makes a negative comment on the internet about another person. The person who is targeted doesn't have the ability to handle the insults and hurts them. The author would suffer an enormous amount of negative reputation regardless of the fact that the legal system may not hold them responsible.

It's much more simple for people to communicate these days thanks to technological advances. Numerous websites online allow us for us to express our opinions in a non-judgmental manner. It is our right to make foolish, inconsiderate or savage speech.

You can post sarcastic or sarcastic remarks in message boards. It's much easy to attack others who hold different opinions on the internet. However, from the perspective of karmic we are accountable for what we say and write. If we are able to share something useful on the internet, then we'll receive the positive karma that comes with our words. If someone is influenced by our advice and act detrimental to themselves or others and others, then we have created a certain amount of negative karma.

Our motives when we speak are crucial. If we speak to provoke anger or anger among other people, we'll receive an increased amount of negative Karma for any harm that is done. If we make a statement that we think is harmless, but we end up having negative consequences, we will receive lesser bad good karma. However when the speech stopped the person from harming themselves and causing harm to others, we will receive many good Karma. If there is nothing positive to say, refrain from speaking in any way.

Listeners and Readers and

What happens if we're at the receiving end of speeches? There are some simple reactions may not even be thought about when they happen. But, certain reactions to sloppy, insincere and harsh remarks could be detrimental. When someone insults us or others that we love We may get angry and be open to anger-filled outbursts. If we're angered, we must consider whether our anger will help solve anything or cause a whole new set of issues. The use of offensive language can provide an opportunity for bad karma either to be manifested or resolved based on what we do.

We could shout at speakers, or even engage in fights in response. These actions could lead us to more trouble, as we may injure us or others, and could cause us to be in trouble in the eyes of law enforcement. Another option to react to insulting remarks is to simply not respond. We consider the threats as bad history We let them speak whatever they want, without causing any upset to us. There are occasions to be vocal, however. If we're criticized in a way that could cause serious harm to our livelihood, it is imperative to defend ourselves. If the speech that is offensive is personal in nature or a joke, we are able to let the incident go. In this allows some bad karma gets resolved and there is no new karma generated.

Other Subjects

The next chapter we'll explore some topics which merit brief discussions. They cover everything from routine things to discussions about the concept of karma, which need to be explored further.

Shopping

The purchase of items we love is okay; we are entitled to spend our hard-earned cash. There are some concerns regarding the manner in which the products we purchase are produced. Things like clothing and electronics could be produced using children's labor or in factories with poor working conditions. The products then would be exported and then sold in stores. Are these products causing us bad luck? No, it's not.

If the product was not specially designed specifically for us, then there is no reason to be concerned. We must be cautious about products that are unique one of a kind or custom-made to custom order. As an example, we may purchase an item that meets our exact specifications and can be made to order in the manner we prefer. In the process of ordering this item it could expose people to risks or hardships. Because of the possibility of harm that we will be suffering, we can expect to receive a certain amount of bad luck based on the amount of suffering we caused. Avoid buying mass-produced products to avoid negative luck.

Praises, Mantras, and Offerings

Many people turn to prayers and mantras when they desire for divine intervention. We can't deny the existence of a greater power however, Karma's law teaches that no one can determine the events that happen to us. Many desires have not been fulfilled. This happens because we think that our desires were fulfilled with the help of the divine power. The responsibility for our fortunate fortunes must be attributed to us. On the other hand, on the other side on the other hand, there is no need to blame the gods for our mishaps that happen to us. Our misfortunes are all caused by us, too. The actions of the past have made the present, while actions of the present make the future.

Therefore, there is no need to make offerings to gods. If the powers of the universe are really strong and compassionate, then why would they require gifts from us to fulfill our desires. A few people go to extraordinary measures to strike a bargain. They promise to do several charitable acts or give some amount. If praying and chanting mantras brings tranquility, keep doing it. For the rest of us It is the right time to cut back or abandon our dependence on the unknown.

We need to trust ourselves to improve our lives. If there was an omnipotent power that could aid people, then there will there would be no suffering on this planet. If the gods are able to help, they must be able to work within the confines of the person's karmic constitution. We aren't able to cook a particular dish or have someone else cook for us, without having the proper ingredients.

Pseudoscience and Superstition

There are many methods that claim to be able to predict the future and provide good luck. Astrology, palmistry and geomancy, physic readings magic charms, voodoo and numerous other methods. The legitimacy of these techniques are debated, but we shouldn't trust them if we know the law of Karma. If the predictions are that we'll have luck with luck or back luck the future of our lives is changing. If we hear that our future is positive, we should not get too comfortable. If we learn that the future is poor, we shouldn't fret too often. Instead, we can go forward with confidence and continue to make good choices.

There aren't any curses, witchcraft, or other evil spells which can hurt us when we have a solid grasp of the concept of the power of karma. No enemies can wish bad luck upon us. They may set up complex rituals and create voodoo dolls but that won't not be a factor. The bad things that happen in our lifetimes are the result of the past's actions only. That means we shouldn't be trying to make bad things occur to people that who we don't agree with. If we purchase a present to someone, but the person isn't happy with the gift, to whom do we give the gift? The negative energy we send to another person is returned to the gift-giver. This is not only a waste of time however, we're creating situations that may bring negative karma as a result of our negative thoughts.

The palmistry, Astrology and physic readings are able to offer accurate predictions for the future , if they are performed by a professional. However, these readings typically don't reflect our present actions. The lines that we hold in our palms do not get fixed at the time of our birth and change as we get older. Astrology is responsible for the significant stars that impact our lives, however it is possible to see millions of other stars interfering with us, and there is there is no way to determine the entire spectrum. If we hear that predictions are foretelling negative events, we must not merely let our fate be the case. We must do our best to avoid the bad outcomes that could be heading our way through creating positive Karma.

Sometimes, the purchase of a charm or an intention we made led to an outcome that was favorable. It's a mistake to think we purchased our luck or that God helped us. The truth is that our positive result was the result of our luck and good luck, and the luck or desire was a part of the process that brought it to fruition. This is the case of putting the cart in front of the horse.

The past was when people living in Asian nations often relied on geomancy, feng shui, or feng shui to boost their fortunes. Feng shui could involve burying loved ones or building structures in good places based on several factors. By using the correct Feng Shui, people can discover luck in their business or personal lives.

One can only discover the most favorable feng shui spots by virtue of good luck and not the reverse. If our good karma will lead us to favorable spots for feng shui but we should be aware that the best conditions could alter. Natural elements can change the location that has excellent feng shui to an area that is not as beneficial or detrimental. A large part of this transformation is based on our present and previous actions and karma. If we keep doing good actions, we will be able to maintain the good energy from Feng Shui, or counteract the negative energy caused by changes in the places.

When we are born in the world, we carry the karmic makeup. There are things that we can influence but not influence. For instance, we could not change our date of birth or location of birth, no matter the actions we take. So, it is possible to find experts who are able to forecast the future of our lives with good level of accuracy based on the information at the start. However, we'll never be able to fully comprehend all the factors that affect us. With the right attitude we won't have to rely on the outside world to have confidence in our future.

Transfer of Karma

Do we have the ability to transfer our good reputation to another? Many people believe that yes. However, the answer is no. Karma isn't a physical item like money, which we can withdraw and give it away at our own discretion. It is certainly not possible to share our bad luck since nobody else would ever take the risk. Since we cannot offer our bad karma away then it is obvious that we cannot give away our good karma. What method could we apply for transferring our bad karma an other human being.

In the past there was the notion that any bad deeds that ancestors committed would bring bad luck for their descendants. In certain nations there are laws that prohibit monetary debts owed to the deceased person from being transferred to a different person. The laws of karma work in the same way. It would be unfair to not be the situation. Every individual is accountable for their personal karmic choices and no sharing or transfer could occur.

If karmic transference is to be logical, it must suggest that we could get away with taking responsibility for our previous actions. You can buy good karma from people as well as pay someone else to accept your bad luck. Karma's law would not be equally applicable to everyone. In addition it is impossible to be acting on behalf of others so that they get the blessings. For instance, we might like to show the family member we love an opportunity to do good deeds. We could go out and give money to charitable organizations using the name of the relative. But, the relative did not perform any act, and any good karma that is created is attributed directly to the individual who performed the act.

Collective Karma

We all know that we each have our own karma, but can we also share karma other people within our circle? It's not possible because sharing karma doesn't happen among living creatures. It is easy to fall for believing in collective karma when we hear about groups of individuals having fun together or suffering through a disaster collectively. For instance, some people have been killed simultaneously in aircraft crashes or natural catastrophes. In contrast, some people have won lotteries and launched successful businesses in tandem.

A more comprehensive justification for collective good karma could be to examine the different countries on the planet. Certain nations are wealthy and advanced. People living in these countries are able to access resources and freedoms that provide them with numerous opportunities. Some countries are poor and are in continuous turmoil. The citizens of these nations are more susceptible to illness and hunger, they frequently rely on the assistance of other people.

The first world countries are wealthy because their citizens decide to carry out a lot of humanitarian acts and peacekeeping missions that create positive Karma for all of society. Third world nations are less fortunate because their people choose to engage in violent or xenophobic acts that create bad karma that affects the entire society. Collectively, more positive morality is created through actions taken in first world nations , and more bad karma is created by the actions of third world countries. It is possible to conclude that people are able to share good luck through their birthplace in first world nations , and participate in bad karma when born in third world countries.

But, the arguments in favor of collective karma fall apart on more careful examination. We find out that karma is a process that operates at an individual basis. For instance, in the case of people who died in aircraft crashes, we have those who were able to survive the tragedy in spite of missing the flight because of their good Karma. The idea of rich nations versus poor nations argument is not working also because we are aware of the an absolute fact that there are people that are suffering in first world countries as well as citizens who are thriving in third world nations.

The notion of collective karma was created because people who have a similar karmic background are often born in the same places and go through similar events. If you've got plenty of good luck, you are likely to be within the company of other people with similar traits, such as an enduring family, modern living as well as a healthy diet and higher education. Therefore, even the fact that collective karma may not exist but we can examine the surroundings to figure out our karmic profile and potential consequences of karmic nature that could happen.

The cessation of Karma

Does karma ever end? It depends on the way you think about the concept of karma. It is possible to argue that karma is never ending since even the smallest idea that comes to mind can create Karma. Thinking of karma this way is a bit extreme as people are forced to go through endless cycles of bad and good fate. Therefore, it is more sensible to conclude that karma is the result of intentions and that is the belief which is widely accepted as being correct.

It is said that karma ceases once intentions have been fulfilled. Names, family friends work, school and many more provide us with an identity. When we receive enough reinforcements we are able to become a part of the identity we have created. The desire to be happy and avoid pain kick off the cycle of karmic repulsion. When we realize that our current existence is only temporary and we begin to let go of self-centered desires. It is possible to continue to perform good deeds, but we do not want something in exchange. The impact can't happen without the cause, thereby ending karma once and all.

Chapter 9: Karma Theory

Oh Lord "Pardon my transgressions. I am an unholy infidel." My Karmas are taking over my mind. Each time I try to control my emotions and it escalates into another form of revenge. I pray, I seek advice from the Maharishis of the highest order who have transcended Karmic influences. I am sorry for all the events that have occurred. The events have multiplied over a long period of time, bringing me to a confusion. Your Maharishi's guidance can help to some extent. At the end of the day you need to discover your inner guidance source that can assist you, safeguard you and help you heal!

Thank you Lord for helping me am experiencing the rushing stream of blue light, engulfing my body and mind, and body. It is possible to hallucinate for positive reasons, such as a gentle blue light covering your body and mind, as your mind manifests the reality. In the event that the speed of your mind is reduced, you'll come nearer to God who is frozen. The imprints you leave on your mind make it more difficult since its intensity will increase the mental dynamics.

It's as easy as the formula in the following...

GOD Force = Man - Karma (Imprints)......(1)

The above equation demonstrates the simple nature of. If you're capable of removing all your karmic influences and impressions, then you'll become one with God. There is no difference between the macro and micro consciousness. It is evident that karma, or imprints, also referred to as imprints, are magnetic strands that are that are stored in the neurons, the genetics, and the organs involved. In simpler terms,"karma" is a thought that is stored with high-quality organs, brain cells as well as genetics and the mind. It is replayed back in the form of thoughts through brain cells, triggering the organs involved. Karma could be good Karma or a bad one based on the harmony of Nature. Any action that is in opposition to Nature is considered to be negative karma, and it must be dealt with in the most fundamental way. It is true that you've built up karmas each minute, and they become a nightmare when you decide to sit every once in a blue moon. How can you suddenly alter the way your mind been functioning? It's not possible on the summer holiday. It must be a part of regular practices. Meditation should be a part of your routine. In the absence of this, there is no chance of utilizing the sixth sense that allows the mind that perceives through the expanding mental state.

A fate will be passed on to the generations via genetics. If you've recorded conflicts in your the mind, it will be recorded in your offspring's mind. They are referred to as Sanchita Karma, which is based on genetic impressions. So, great care should be taken when recording through the mind since it is recorded within the micro and macro consciousness. The events that are recorded by the cosmos as well as your genetics will attract similar forces to alter your Karma's. Your goal in life involves aligning your body with the higher consciousness through the dissolution of the karmas from your past and present. These are called the sanchita and Prarabdha Karma. The akamiya karma's are ones you perform in your current life. They're similar to chain reactions because you're affected by the sanchita karma which leads you to a specific mind, and then you'll be able to see all the world with the lenses of your mind, leading to an additional study that might or may not be in line with universal laws. This leads you to the sequence of events that are meticulously recorded. When you consider something is registered and remain in active for 120 years after the date you registered. Thus the reason why our Yogis have described the time to think as seven janmas. 7X20 = 140 years is the time span of every thought you've recorded. If you register again you will get all the life time of the day you registered it. Therefore that our Genetic scientists are discovering magnetic DNA strands to treat ailments in offspring. It is a huge task to transform the carmic pattern. It is easy and achievable to overcome the karmas that are already in place by engaging in deep communication with the super-conscious and an analysis of your own can assist you in drawing a more extensive line that will nurture positive thinking and assist in helping your negative thinking to sublimate. It's also simple to get to the root of your emotions and understand the source of the problem through self-conselling. This can help alleviate the negative belief. If the thought of negative thoughts occurs, you won't be a target for attention as you think rationally and think subliminally without being affected by the state of mind that affects your emotions.

The majority of Karmic patterns arise from inattention. There's always the option to carry out an action with the senses in a state of consciousness or even without paying attention. This could result in an inconsistent pattern since you've not made use of your the mind to be able to keep a record of an event with precise manner. As an example. You're listening to music or having food or sex after getting drunk. Now, the conflicting pattern will emerge. After you have recovered from the state of sobriety, you'd have exhausted your energy and felt no satisfaction. Therefore, it is important to be aware of the act that it's written down in your brain and the super-conscious mind. If it's reflecting on itself, you'll face problems because you've not recorded it in a precise manner.

These Karmic patterns are recorded with high-quality at a specific speed, i.e. the mental frequencies that is in cycles per second. It is possible to recall it in the form of thoughts that are virtual anytime, provided you let your mind shift to a level of frequencies. The goal should be to keep the mental frequency as minimal as is possible to protect yourself from impressions of the karmic. One of the things you should be aware of is recording the mind and should be done with a gentle frequency when you are that is in a state where you are aware. The second part is reflecting that you shouldn't expose the mind's frequency to an higher level, which could cause you to become attuned to an altered state, as well as the similar forces that exist in the universe. Your mind may be attuned to the wavelengths listed below for example, tuning FM radio

* Beta (14-40 Cps),

* Alpha (7-13 Cps),

*Theta (3-6 Cps) and

* Delta (0-2 Cps)

God is the state of zero in terms of potential energy and 2 or 3 Cps in the state of dynamic. If you can reach the state of mind that is the lowest that is, you'll be tuning with your God force. The closer you get, greater your spiritual growth. The pleasures you indulge in could increase your mental frequency to fifteen Cps and up to around 40 Cps. If you go beyond 40 Cps your cells will collapse in a heart attack like it occurs to someone who is in a severe state of emotional turmoil in anger. The heart ceases to function after this point since it cannot fulfill the demands of the cells , which are operating at a rapid pace because of the agitated emotional state. Your mind is a wave. This wave is generated from the whirling of energy particles. The life force particle, or sub-atomic particles are generated from the sexual vital fluid. It's essential to keep good supply of sexual vital fluid in order to make use of the energy for spiritual practices.

The quantity and quality of your sexual vital fluid can determine the state of mind. It is important to be aware of your sexual vital fluid. It's isn't fun to lose vital fluid because of negative thoughts, excessive fantasies and unmoral sexual desire. If sexual vital fluid becomes lost, the cells disappear and become phony, losing their vitality and potential. In the end, it will lose its ability to build up immune system against disease. The body's immune system will start to lose its immunity and be more susceptible to illnesses.

Your behavior is a result of the recordings. You've been practicing a particular kind of behavior, like eating food, having sexual activity. This pattern is formed in your mind . The pattern will continue until you attempt to become aware of these situations to alter your destructive behaviour. There's nothing wrong with basic instincts as that you don't go out of your way to been able to enjoy it in moderate amounts. Any excess can cause addiction, and leave negative impressions. Once you've become accustomed to a particular activity in brain cells, and orgains, it's going to remain even if you'd prefer to alter it after a while. It's like having an self-contained recording device that records events in a precise manner. If you're young, it will be simple to mould your mind to follow a certain patterns that yield benefits. This is precisely the way that each Religion tried to do but did not succeed due to lack of scientific investigation, which leads to the condition of despair among the young generation. It is essential to investigate every incident scientifically, and analyze the causal and resulting factors before it's imprinted. It is essential to prevent negative outcomes of imprints.

Your mind is a powerful recording machine and you'll have to manage it with care and the state of consciousness. Meditation is the best way to bring your mind into the consciousness. The quality of consciousness would be an integral to your consciousness if your meditation practices are profound enough to allow you to see your own self-awareness and to align your mind with the macro consciousness.

The majority of the initial set of karmic imprints is passed down to you, and then you take action on it, creating experiences, feelings as the another set of imprints. It is then incorporated into your character as well as your behavior and eventually your character. Therefore, every religion tries to instill good habits at an early age in order to cleanse your past, and simplifying your karmic patterns. In the present World there's an easier way to market women and men due to the proliferation of mass media, like Internet and satellite channels broadcasting. The constant training process that your brain undergoes and you've lost your uniqueness and the ability to think, think rationally and grow into a genuine and true personality. Because of this conditioning, there's an increasing number of crimes against women and other women because your sexual power has become poisoned to the roots. If you look at your data carefully the sensations you experience, you will realize that every one of them resulted from need has been sold as a product to satisfy your desires. For instance. The need for food has been overemphasized by the wide many different foods and the same is the case with sexual sex. It is impossible to keep your stomach full or take pleasure in sexual intimacy beyond the limits of your body and the energy levels. Because your brains are programmed, there is always a desire for more with the senses and perceptions are your primary focus because you've never realized you're observing reality through your sixth sense. This is an expanding mental state.

A disturbed and conditioned mind could lead to issues in the adult years like schizophrenia, ADHD and halllucination type of disorders. The mind's conflicts will expand if not addressed at the simplest level. The most effective alternatives is to break free of your mind and free it from continuous meditation and analysis, as a daily practice which will erase the negative impressions that have been left on you, thereby decreasing the negative effects of spiritual influences. The reason is because your mind is recording continuously in every single second, whether you are comfortable with the idea or not. If you don't are diligent about clearing your mind daily as a routine, it can be difficult to get rid of the accumulation of imprints. It's like a pile trash that you put away for years in your backyard. Imagine the effort required to wash it over night ....and what will happen to it. It's so dirty and unsanitary, it's a suffocating feeling isn' it? Similar thing happens to your mind when it's not kept clean and maintained regularly. This can lead to various mental illnesses and splits that can lead to an illness that lasts forever as your mind's energy is a control for your the body.

Your body could be vulnerable to a variety of illnesses. Then, you'd go insane by taking a suicide decision or perhaps inviting all sorts of bodily and mental illnesses. The body serves as a shrine. On the other side of your mind is the GOD force that has manifested in your. If you don't pay attention enough to remove yourself from spiritual imprints that have been left on you, you'll never be able to achieve success in your endeavor.

It is much simpler to look at your patterns of karmic behavior at the age of a child and change your behavior in line with them. It is possible to escape your struggles and be in charge of your present circumstance and past events by using your brain. Each of these studies requires a great deal of effort to analyze the imprints, superimpose it and break them down during meditation. If you're delaying it until the end of your career, then your karmic patterns will increase at times, based on the chance to dissolve. For instance. For instance, anger and Immoral love for sex are examples of karmic patterns derived of the fundamental instincts. You'd have lived a simple life in the world but you've never examined it at the deepest level and attempted to discern it through the sixth sense, in an expanded states of mind. If you attempt to look at your life when you're sixty, you've already automated the cells to act according to the karmic pattern and suddenly it is impossible to alter your behaviour. It's true that your dog's behavior won't change when they get old. It is not possible to chase the tail, as your life will become useless and meaningless if you weren't in control of your karmic habits.

It's possible to watch all in the pattern of karmic karma play the spoil sport , and it manifests into moments of pleasure or pain. If it's bad karma then you're going to be in trouble.s Many times there are people who are working. They'll find it difficult to meditate on their own and analyze their Karmic patterns when they reach an older age. Therefore, these practices need to begin at the around 14 years old. Once you are able to comprehend the concepts that your life will grow into a multiverse of the form of benediction, and meditation will soon be immersed in cosmic consciousness, with dissolving Karmic patterns. Everything is imprinted with precision such as the way you eat food, how you are sexually active and the way you dream. Everything is imprinted as hereditary impressions. If you are able to cleanse to a certain extent your progency, it will evolve into an enlightened state of mind quickly. The life-history artifacts of saints of the highest order like Buddha, Maharishi Vethathiri, Bodhi Dharma show that the majority of them have been born with the initial series of imprints, which are clean, and not needed from the souls of the Enlightened. They had nevertheless studied hard and delved into the initial imprints, and asked relevant questions about themselves in order to grow into the eternal mind.

It's ironic that you're struggling to transcend the ordinary world of existence due to a conditioned mind that has definite patterning of karmic nature. The initial set of patterns will affect your personality. Now, imagine you're drunk. What happens?

Your neurons are disconnected and your brain is unable to communicate with your brain. The mind is the ultimate recording or replaying machine. It will record every conflicting pattern of what you see through your senses. Every single moment, experience result, pleasure or even what you consider to be enjoyment with only the limited perception of your brain will be recorded with precise detail. It's like an Operah show that was recorded using an unprofessional recording. The output will not be as good, is it? Similar to the analogy above the output of these recordings are stored inside your unconscious mind, and will be transferred to the conscious whenever a similar environment arises, resulting in multiple stands of contradicting patterns that are stored in brain cells. In the end, you will never be able rationalize these thoughts. What's important is that you're also losing your awareness when you're drunk and the re-cording of your brain will become erratic, leading to neurologic disorders and the emergence of false sensations, leading to addictions. It's impossible to even enjoy regular sex once you've had a drink since your limbs, sexual glands and brain cells won't work in tandem , leading to early discharge. You'll be lose energy and eventually becoming addicted to the sex because you're unhappy with. The cycle will continue until you get out of the cycle. Take note!

Be aware of the karmic cumulative impressions that result from habits that lead you to discord with Nature. If you smoke, drink or drink your neurons will go inert, filling the system with contradicting patterns that are recorded in your our minds. In the event that it replays you'll be uneasy and it'll be difficult to ignore. Therefore, the hallucinations are present. You are aware of how difficult it is to fight cancer. The reason is because the cells being unable to grow. One reason could be the excessive release in sexual vital fluid that leads to cells becoming void and losing their charge. These types of karmic patterns could be present in all of us, even if they are not recognized in the early stages. There are ways to minimize the dangers of genetic impressions in the early stages through a harmonious lifestyle in sync with Nature.

I'd suggest you become conscious next time you smoke or drink to look at your body, mind, and mind in a holistic way instead of having anyone helping you comprehend.

The extent to which you're causing damage to your body and mind. Subatomic particles spin at an extremely high speed that causes an excessive loss of bio-energy (magnetism). The senses of your brain are affected and your neurons will be severely damaged because of the heat produced. Additionally, these patterns get replicated in your body's cells, genes and brain cells, too. Even if you're not drunk following a regular drinking pattern over time your cells could react differently after you've accelerated and conditioned your cells.

Each of these cells is equipped with its own mind, which is responsible for recording events in a precise manner. So, you must put an end to any further karmic pattern because of smoking, drinking or any other behaviour such as sexual conduct. In the event that you do not, all of those imprints will be your first set of karmic attributes that will be registered to your offprints. The weak progeny will go throughout his life for sublimating the Karmic effects through the physical and mental realm to dissolving every one of these. Additionally, these karmic imprints will extend based on the incidents and actions, thoughts, sequences and patterns that are experienced by him throughout his lifetime based by the initial generation of genetic imprints. The next generation of your children will be able to dissolve N+1 imprints. Imagine that your next generation would contain a plethora of KARMIC imprints to dissolve and keep increasing until you stops, re-visit the analysis and search for an eternal awareness to help your. There is a way to dissolve in a single generation, by diligently doing yoga, meditation and contemplative analysis. Each of these practices will restore the cells affected by hereditary imprints. For instance. A person is more likely of developing diabetes due to their father's. In the present, one can engage in exercises, and adopt healthy food habits that will help to align the cells. Although he is likely to develop diabetes, he will be able to alter and restore the cell structure so that he can lead an active and healthy life. In the same way, behaviors of smoking or drinking, as well as sexual indiscretions can be controlled through proper meditative practices prior to they cause major health issues for you, such as sexually transmitted diseases, cancer and other diseases.

It is well known that prevention is more effective than curing. What are you going to do if WHO predicts a very large numbers of heart disease and brain cell damage caused by stress at a young age around 35 years old is a shock to comprehend. All of these are due to emotions that can be inherited or triggered by you due to your environment, food, habits and social interactions. It is important to think about the cause and eliminate any harmful behavior. It is therefore essential to get started on an analysis of your harmful behavior by conducting periodic chart analyses of your mental frequency in order to reduce your negative behaviors. What's the benefit of building wealth on your own at the cost to your health?, broken relationships. It is important to prioritize everything in order to ensure your well-being. Your work shouldn't be a burden on your body. If it creates a huge stress on your body, then either shift jobs or stop allowing yourself to the stress through the art of observing. Otherwise, you'd end up spending your hard-earned money in the hospitals. Most of these patterns are multiplied due to your actions or reverting to the base set of karmic characteristics. The pattern slowly grows and causes ripples within your mind, body. If you are addicted to substances such as alcohol and smoking, you'll be unable to make progress on this path of studying your karmic patterns. I would like to ask everyone to quit drinking because it is a detriment to your neurons and senses. After a certain period neurons begin to become inactive and will not be able to coordinate with the sensory. Your life will be filled with hallucinations. Even if you're not drinking you'll be experiencing hallucinations throughout the day and night which can cause neurological problems, and prolonged drinking can cause heart disease as well as other health issues.

There are three types of Karmas:

1. Sanchita Karma - These are your genetic imprints, and your first set of traits.

2. Prarabdha Karma This is the self thoughts, actions, activities based on the initial set of traits (sanchita karma)

3. Acamiya Karma - Thease are your actions that leave imprints on the soul.

The latest addition in my mind is virtual Karma. These are just your imaginations and are not a real incident based on all kinds of addicitons on the television, internet or mobile phones, fbook. etc.

Laws of Karma

Energy is in the process of transformation. Your thoughts, mind and brain are nothing more than streams of energy..either either kinetic or potential. It's always evolving and trying to release its power. According to the explanation the karmas you have are thoughts and events that are gespeichert in the brain's cells genes organs, minds cells, and the universal consciousness in patterns precise. It is stored in knots or magnetic strands and is inactive for 120 years. It is able to play back to human being, after many several years with high-quality. The quality of karmic influence are determined by how well they are recorded made by Mind. If you've recorded in a state that is conscious that is, then the result will be excellent results. If, however, you recorded in a state that is confusion, insanity, or in a state of emotion the karmic influence would bring you into an uneasy state. Since these patterns of karmic influence are stored as magnetic strands, each single moment is recorded without any amount as dots in the cells of your body and your life force. The life force you have is called atma or the soul that will continue to exist in the absence of the physical body. Even if your body ceases to exist your atma will continue to be carrying these imprints until it totally sublimates to nothing. When it has sublimated all imprints, it becomes part of Universal consciousness. The purpose of the life force is to cleanse its human consciousness and grow through connection with the eternal consciousness, and to become in harmony with God. Divine Nature. This is the sole goal of life, and human beings are blessed with the senses that allow us to comprehend our nature, grow from animal species through reasoning, learning, and thinking with the mind, that is known as the sixth sense, and grow into the eternal truth by the process of purifying the impressions. All of life is a useless in the pursuit of happiness by pursuing sensual pleasures , because it's impossible to expand beyond the limitations of our senses. There's nothing wrong with the pleasures of sensuality, but you must be aware of its limitations before you can evolve to eternal truth and joy.

Karma's laws can aid you in understanding it in more depth:

The Laws of Karma:

1. Every action has an equal reaction

a. Karmas can cause joy or pain based on the cause and the effects system.

2. Karma, an electromagnetic shadowwave that originated in Mind to storage of energy in precise

3. The Kinematics of Karma is influenced by Time Distance, Volume, and Force

4. Karma is an example of chain reaction

5. Your karmas that cause the self or society with pain is thought as a negative belief that causes discord with Nature

6. Your karmas may lead towards the state of Universe through the sixth sense (super conscious mind) or revert to the condition of conditioned mind illusion

7. Your karmas could be a source of an energy source in the genetic center, and then passed on to offspring

Karmic influences are extremely strong and could be a tidal wave anytime, based on their magnitude. Therefore, it must be maintained, cleansed and observed regularly, like clearing your dinner plate. It's cumbersome and it is impossible to carry around a massive laundry bag since the list of laundry items is growing every day. If you are able to clean it regularly it will be easy to focus and open your mind's awareness. It's possible you're not conscious of your personality's core as well as the conditioned mind, and karmic influences from genetics and own design. Each of these elements need to be examined in order to comprehend the karmic influences you have that lie hidden within the subconscious mind. It is possible to remove them each one at a time in complete silence. There's no other way to discern because you'll need a great deal of strength to eliminate the negative karmic influence. If you let them be to be as they are, each of them would be transferred from the subconscious mind to the conscious mind upon the relativistic variables such as distance, time as well as volume and force. For instance. The fears you had as a child could turn into anxiety in the adult years and your inexperience about sexuality as a teenager could have far greater effects on your sexual life, which can lead to disorders. So, you must be aware of your influence from time to the moment as they can have influence on your personality. Your beliefs, opinions and perceptions within your mind are subjective to the karmic and baseline conditioning influences.

Maybe, you haven't been paying attention to it. The untreated thoughts, emotions, and karmas/thoughts that are conditioned could cause chaos at any point in your life if the issue is not dealt with from the root. Karmic imprints may be hidden as they require a particular mental state of frequency of thought or energy level to develop. If it develops into your mind in the form of thoughts, it can trigger numerous unpleasant hallucinations, like spider webs that repeats itself.

You can either elevate your self-esteem or decrease your life force via the way you think. They are similar to energy bubbles that are forming in the form of energy packets through the subconscious into the consciousness. If you're awake that you are, you'll be able see it as one after another and release these thoughts through self-councel. Each of these energy strands will guide you, and even protect you, and protect you. This reduces the negative effects resulting from the negative thoughts. The impact of negative impressions can manifest through the body as illnesses and mental conflicts. Every time, you'll experience a mental conflict.

Law #1

"For every action, there is An equivalent response"

This is the cause and effect structure of Universal rules of Nature. Nature operates with pattern accuracy, regularity and precision throughout everything from the smallest atom all the way to the massive planets. The variety of manifestations of energy are subject to cause and effect system. It is impossible to have any effect without a reason somewhere. "You cannot pick an iris, and not disturb an unobserved star". Therefore, if you behave in a state of emotional or in a state of ignorance or in a state of naivety, every thought or actions would be a sure way to draw attention to events in accordance with the laws of Nature. For instance. When you shake your hands, you is sound because of the conversion of pressure wave into sound. The analogy applies to your thoughts. All thoughts are stored like a within your brain cells. The thought will trigger the frequency of your mind. If it is activated it will produce results that are accelerated by cells that can organize an event, or to rely on thoughts.

Most of the time the thoughts, actions, outcomes of experience, joy of results, research, conclusion of an moment are already stored with the highest quality. If you're smart enough to look over the entire sequence of events, you're alerting your mind to sublimate the thought on the outcomes as positive or negative. If you're allowing these thoughts to be interpreted as joy or sadness because of your habitual mind and your mind is allowing it to perceive the pleasure or pain in relation to the energy levels. If your energy in the mind is lost beyond a point and your mind is aware of it, you will perceive it as suffering or, if it's within boundaries, your mind is able to perceive that it is a pleasure. In both cases, the sensations of pleasure and pain are experienced by the conscious mind, based on the utilization by your biological magnetic force. It is essentially a transformation of energy. Therefore, you must realize that every one of these feelings of pleasure and pain are simply the result of an exchange of the mental energy lost by the different senses.

Similar to the cost of sexual vital fluid can be recognized by the mind as pleasure, but an addiction or conditioned brain would be tempted to seek it out. If your sexual vital fluid has been diminished in excess, or you are sexually thoughts could lead to dissolving the vital fluid decreasing the overall quality of the mind. So, you must be aware of enjoying with moderation when engaging in the senses. Additionally, you should be extremely cautious when using your senses and follow a five-point strategies in the following aspects and not go over the limit:

Food, rest, sexual working and the usage of thoughts. If you are over the limit that you are able to reach, your mind, thinking process can be altered, leading to mental disorders and additional stimulation for the sensory system. If you're addicted to pleasures of the sensual, your body is likely to follow cell's mind instead of the central consciousness and suffer the consequences of exhausted energy. This could lead to a state of desperation or mental depression, mental split, and illnesses in the body.

Law #2

"Karma is an electromagnetic wave that originated in Mind Transfer energy"

Mind is Wave, and your thoughts are ripples. Every action, thought or thought is recorded as an event through the windows that is the senses. For instance. When you're looking at a gorgeous parrot, your eyes will observe and it transforms into a dot , and then it is an electrical strand within the brain cells that have characteristics that are characteristic of the parrot, such as shape, color and so on. Your brain stores this information with precise detail through the eyes inside brain cells. If you ever reflect on the parrot that you saw, your brain will recreate it in a precise manner. Additionally, every recording has an appropriate frequency. Watching an animal could have been recorded with Beta frequency (14-30 Cps) however, it was not be in an anxious state of mind so you'd feel relaxed when you think about the incident. However, if you're contemplating an accident, your body's cells will be excited, which can cause anxiety. This is due to over-exuberant mental energy that has been diminished by the mind force. Therefore, it is important to be aware of and understand the nature of thinking. Your mind can take forms, but it is limited to the laws of force volume, time, and distance. In the analogy above, recording a parrot's event is constrained by force time as well as size (shape) as well as distance. Each recording will produce a particular magnetic field across the body, stimulating the cells. Lastly, bioprints are also performed within the Genetic center, and then passed on to the children.

If you're collecting karmas which cause negative reactions to the body's chemistry, bio-magnetism and organs because of conflicts with Nature The result will be pain the majority times. So, you must be aware of the events that cause pain in your life and make plans to remove these negative karmic effects. Your genetic center may have thousands of negative karmas as a result of the following causes:

1. Food,

2. Negative thinking

3. Conflicts in the mind because of ignorance of every aspect,

4. Unfulfilled desires,

5. Planetary movement

All of the factors listed above must be thoroughly assessed. You'll have to take a deep look to identify any harmful behaviors. If you let your mind wander, it could create a myriad of desires that will not lead you to the Divine. It is important to examine your eating habits and opt for an aperitif or vegetarian diet to ensure your body is healthy. If you're eating non-vegetarian foods then you're bringing on your karmas, such as fears, emotions, which are the animal instincts. If you're constantly surrounded by negative thoughts because of unintentional films, or the internet, your brain is likely to stimulate. This can lead to different patterns, which can cause negative mind set, which results in depleted mental energy. Thirdly, the reason for mind conflicts is because of recording events without analyzing it. For instance. It is possible to record an incident within your emotional state or in a state of ignorance. Some people believe that drinking, smoking or fantasies about sexuality is enjoyable and enjoyment. This can lead to negative karma that causes conflicts. Each time it rises up, your mind will judge it as a negative experience, causing disturbance to your brain and your mental enery flow. The mind-body conflict cannot be resolved until you discover the root of the sensations, find the correct ones, and assure yourself that it is just an idea. Otherwise , it will saturate your mental energy to the point of which can lead to a state of despair due to the maladies that plague the body. Additionally, unfulfilled or desires which are developed to gain the highest amount of material wealth and sexual desires that go over and above the urge to eat and so on can lead to miserable lives because these desires are not fulfilled. The only option is to take self-care and recognize these destructive behaviors and to superimpose on a positive karma through means of services, meditation to dispel negative karmic influence.

Law #3

"The The Kinematics behind Karma is based in Time, Distance, Volume and Force."

Your mind is a wave, which is bound by four variables that are that is, a) Time, the second) Distance and c) Volume, and the fourth one is) Force. Its origin is due to friction between the whirling particles of force and the space inside your body. The body is composed of three layers: three layers: a) Physical body comprised of cells) Astral body composed by life force particles, and the third layer is) Causal body that is the body that is magnetic. It's all energy phenomena.

Your karma can be described as an event stored in the cells as well as consciousness. What is recorded in cells has a specific frequency. If you can tune your thoughts to the frequency and then the karmic effects are a result of the subconscious mind. These karmic patterns could be a result of your personal karma, or may be derived result from genetics. It is important to maintain your mind in an lower frequency in order to stay clear of negative influences. The problem is that you multiply karmas by relying on the first pattern of karmic frequencies. They are cumulative and go in the direction of compounding into billions of magnetic strands that are meticulously recorded. Perpahs, these designs are constructed to aid you in understanding the Nature within your own mind and expand your horizons. When the sixth sense isn't used, then humans are bound to live a life of suffering due to repetitive patterns that produce similar negative outcomes.

Your sexual energy is the basis. It creates billions of subatomic particles that create a magnetic circuits a.k.a bio-magnetism in your body. It is essential to learn of the science behind energy. The pleasures you experience in your body are an expense for a particular quantities in biomagnetic power. Sexual activity is thought to be a sign of happiness because the brain is activating and the entire body experiences a sensation of joy when you release seminal fluid. This is thought to be an act of Divine act when you are aware of the science behind. It will assist you to expand beyond and transcend sexual energy to spirituality. This is good luck charm as long as your excessive sexual vital fluid is released to your partner in a respectful manner. This is completely religious and divine. If you find yourself craving it, and become addicted to the practice, this becomes a problem, and irreligious. It is vital to keep an adequate quantity and quality of sexual vital fluid in order to assist in building up immunity against the disesase process at an age, which is greater than 40. If you are releasing it too much to satisfy your desires without knowing the facts, it could cause serious damage to your brain cells, and the organs. In the end, when your semen is fluid and non-existent, the entire physiology is susceptible to all kinds of ailments. The medical journals have not been able to clarify the importance of the sexual vital fluid and have not been able to comprehend the subatomic particles produced from the fluid. I wish there would come an era when science will recognize these truths of Siddha's as well as Buddha's. It's a science that is simple.

If you're imagining, then the entire sequence is recorded with negative karmic effects creating a myriad of mental disturbances. There is no way to erase negative imprints of virtual reality by taking actions. It's like trying to find an invisible shadow. You can't find it since it doesn't exist. If you bring it into the consciousness of light, it will vanish. You have to harness your vitality towards spirituality by being responsible, absorbing the science of energy , and improve your meditation and introspective analysis. There are kaya kalpa techniques taught world wide by the www.vethathiri.edu.in centers across the Globe. These practices will allow you to get rid of the karmic influences and recognize your place within this life. The Divine Nature is the best This is a blessing! !

A mind that wanders is a devil's workbench.. Your karmic patterns can affect your mental, physical and emotional wellbeing.

Therefore, it's important to acknowledge your karmic influences as early as you can to remove them as swiftly as is possible. Once you've removed the obstacles in your life, you'll be in a position to open the gates to heaven.

Law # 4

"Karma is the result of a chain reaction."

It's similar to an unidirectional chain reaction. Karmas can be acquired as part of your hereditary imprints. This is the initial sequence of karma-related characteristics. You then began constantly increasing your karma without thinking about it with your intellect. It will be obvious by looking at the previous behavior and the effects of suffering or peace. In the event that you're guilty of been committing a negative act, it indicates that you've created a lot of negative karma's and impacting your response to events. These are prarabdha-karmas that can lead to actions in moment. The burden will be a burden to your mind if you do not release it. Then, your mind will split and scatter all negative thoughts one after another. You could have put off listening to these songs by engaging yourself in some kind of activity.

What happens following retirement? After you retire, you can sit back and lay back and relax. It will be difficult to rest as each karma will grow one after the next as if a nuclear chain reaction. In the beginning, it triggers an alteration in the chemical balance of your body, which results in an imbalance of harmone. In addition, it affects the organs and physiology all at a time, making your body vulnerable to many ailments. The immune system will decrease. Therefore, karma isn't solely affecting the mental realm of the mind. It also affects biological processes of the cells by altering their structure and energy levels.

Now, you are conscious of the karmic influence. There are yoga practices to help you rebalance the body's cells that are affected through the pattern of karmic influence that affects the organs you are relying on. It is important to take a check for your levels of harmone (TSH) as well as sugar levels, to know the extent to which your body is affected by the Karmic pattern. It could be inherited or even your own creation. The way you think has to be at their best. If you're stressed out on the mental level this could affect the physical body, too.

What happens when you drink from a an arma-based perspective? I'd like each one of you to take a look and reflect on the following issues.

Drinking alcohol, level of blood sugar will rise. When alchohol is introduced into the bloodstream it weakens the coordination between hearts and cells. The hyphothalamus of your heart is deactivated which means that the brain cells will receive mixed and contradicting messages. The messages that are transmitted to brain cells aren't necessarily the correct ones. Second, if the neurons in the brain are not active then you will experience hallucinations without conscious thought. That is one of the more risky Karma that is accumulated through virtual sensations. Ecstacy-like sensations are not natural as you'd be able to hallucinate. It's like having a dream of sex forever as if floating through the sky. The karma that you experience is etched as a magnetic knot in brain cells, which transmit conflicting messages. Morso If you're awake and trying to stay aware, these thoughts would be so wildly contradictory that you'd want to block it because you know it's not the right one in the awakefulness state of your mind. Since you've recorded it in an uninvolved state the mind will try to replay the recording every time. The result is that your brain would trigger your brain cells that become over-heated due to the conflicting patterns. Your mental energy would diminish, and you will feel depleted of energy, tired , and eventually you'll go to sleep. This will be reflected in your nightmares. If you drink frequently will have severe consequences both in their body and the mind. Karmic patterns of negative nature would appear as large as is possible from the unconscious mind and into the conscious mind. The paradox is the fact that this karmic pattern could be revealed in the morning, when you're awake. Try to sit down and meditate. They will come out, making you feel like you're in the state of confusion! So, it is important be aware of your behavior or smoking, and drinking for friendship. Each is a permanent mark on the body cells, the mind brain cells, and organs involved in the process of drinking or smoking cigarettes, having excessive thoughts, or sexual activity. All of these are recorded with exactness.

Alarming, isn't. Don't you worry. There's always an option to get out. These karmic patterns you've created can be wiped out with a positive behaviour. A person who is addicted alcohol or smoking cigarettes can choose alternative actions like taking orange juice, or even smoking a herb cigar. Etc. In the same manner the person that is addicted sexual activity needs to be aware of the changes in energy within himself as well as the science and anatomy of reproductive and female organs to break free from his own self.

Law # 5

"Your Karmas that cause hurt on your self or the society are thought to be negative karmas that cause discord with Nature"

What is the definition of a Karma? You've probably guessed it is an act or event that is recorded as an impression. It could be carried out at any moment in your life depending on the conditions. They are stored within your Genetic center and replayed back by the brain cells and organs, causing a disturbance in your cells known as pain. Good karma can result in no disruption in your body or mind which will result in peace. Maybe you've recorded while in the state of emotional turmoil or are unsure of an event that caused conflicting patterns to be that are stored as magnetic knots in neurons in your brain and in the genetics. When you're awake, you're not aware but your mind records every moment. If you're conscious you will be recorded in the same way. It's like using a quality or poor recorder to record an event. If you're using an inferior microphone, then the quality of your recording will be poor isn't it. Similar thing happens to your brain. If you're recording in a state of semi-consciousness, the quality of the recording you make inside your head would be low, which could result in an inconsistent pattern.

Your mind is a wave therefore it is a wave. It lets go of all the karmic impressions one after another. You must be aware, do a quick exercise to look at your thoughts. It will become more conscious over time. When your mind's power is improved, you will be you will be immune to the karmic influences. It's like when the body's way of defending itself against destructs. In the same manner the mind's immunity through mind will assist you in overcoming negative karmic patterns and assist to completely erase these impressions. Otherwise , you'd see each karmic thought coming out of your unconscious mind one after the next and taking you of your energy. It could result in thousands of problems in life which you'll never be able to conquer because your life will get increasingly complicated and stressful. Instead, you should be strong in your mind, you can build it through practice. You won't be able to shake yourself. The karmic patterns disappear over some time, as you're not hosting them. The pattern will eventually it difficult to break.

Law # 6

"Your beliefs can bring you towards the universe's state Universe through six sense (super conscious mind) or even revert back into the realm of conditioned brain in the state of delusion"

You've documented many of these events within a semi-conscious brain in accordance with your own conditioned mind. For instance. The fantasies and sexual fantasies are result of your recordings in a semi-conscious states or after a drinking, which can result in numerous hallucinations. These desires are all unconscious patterns that are not subject to proper analytical and rational thinking. which means that you're not using your sixth sense that is able to think expand and align itself with the eternal mind. What you record with your mind that is in a semi-conscious state could result in negative outcomes. It's as easy to record events with cameras that aren't good. However, when you're using a higher resolution and high quality camera to record your events, it's a perfect choice, isn't?

In the same way the mind must be free of any conditioning first. If it can be aligned with your conscious mind to record events that are based on the third dimension, then your life will be transformed to your advantage. This is that siddhas and saints are discussing. Being aware and conscious. If you're aware of your thoughts, your reasoning will be clear and unclouded. These events would be recorded in a non-contradictory patterns, leading to an alignment to the cosmic consciousness.

It may be of the result of your own choice or passed down from your family's collection of traits. A good karma is one that is in harmony with Nature with no disturbances while a negative karma the one that conflicts with Nature and lead to a quagmire and diseases of the body and mind, as well as confusion that can lead to various ailments and mental afflictions.

Additionally, you know that negative karmic patterns that are present in the body can be eliminated through superimpose techniques and cells can be aligned correctly through the practice of Yoga. Your drinking habits will eventually cause problems for your the physiology as well as mentally. It reduces the mental energy and the phsyicalatomic structure, which causes severe damage to organs. If you're drinking your liver will be exhausted and will attempt to remove alcohol from your bloodstream. The demands put on cells will be alarmingly increased and cause stress to your heart.

In essence, you are impairing your liver, heart cells, brain cell, body cells, magnetic energy, and life force circuits within your body. These patterns of karmic repercussions are registered throughout your body and passed on into your kids. Additionally, if a single kind of karma is tracked within the consciousness of cosmic nature. This will cause further trouble. Nature manifests into situations to remove this karma via individuals, events that are projected around your body, and events that are projected around you. This is a Universal truth. You can't claim that another person is right, since you've provoked wrath through your actions that resulted into karmic patterns formed within your.

Law # 7

"Your Karmas could be a source of energy stored within the genetic center and passed on to offspring"

Conclusion

Congrats on reaching the conclusion to this book! I'd like to let everyone know that once more that you're in control in your personal life. No one is forcing you to be miserable. Nobody is holding a gun to your head and telling for you to feel powerless. You're the one who did it.

It hurts to hear. It's not easy however the quicker you can get your head about that fundamental fact and accept it, the faster you'll have the ability to regain control to control your destiny.

When you assert your ownership over your life and affirm to yourself that you have done this to myself, and I'm able to do something different for myself, that is the moment that you've broken the rules of freedom.

I would like you to experience this freedom and strive to achieve the results I believe you can achieve. Whatever you consider your role model and what you believe in, if they are able to accomplish it, you could achieve it as well.

Do not let anyone believe otherwise. There is no limit to your potential. Be aware of the fact. Get started taking action on the ideas I've discussed in this book so that you can live your best life.

Wishing you nothing more than joy, happiness as well as love and happiness.

www.ingramcontent.com/pod-product-compliance
Lightning Source LLC
Chambersburg PA
CBHW050404120526
44590CB00015B/1828